Preface

C000147208

It is not surprising that there are a ᴵᴼᵗ ᴼᶠ ᵇᵃᵗᵗˡᵉᶠⁱᵉˡᵈˢ ⁱⁿ ᵗʰᵉ Midlands. As opposing armies converged on each other from different parts of the country, it is logical that they should often meet up somewhere in the centre. The Midlands has thus played a prominent part in the military history of England and the events that form the basis of the 22 walks in this guide range in time from the 13th to the 20th century.

Walking battlefield sites is a most rewarding and pleasurable experience. The following selection stretches over a large and varied area and includes both urban and rural walks. As well as providing exercise and fresh air, these walks arouse historic interest and stimulate the imagination. At times a great deal of imagination is required as there is often little to see on the ground and it is difficult to envisage the site at the time of the battle. The chief problem is that battlefields are not protected in the same way as ancient buildings. At the time of the battles most were used for agricultural purposes and this has continued. In more recent times some of them have been built on and have modern road and railways running across them. Some are inaccessible because there are no public rights of way across them, although in all cases they can be viewed from adjacent roads, lanes or footpaths. Only a few have well-signed 'Battle Trails' or visitor centres. The nearest that they have to any protection is that English Heritage has a register of over 40 of the most historic battlefields and offers advice to owners, planners and other interested groups on ways to conserve and enhance these sites and to encourage greater public access.

Despite these limitations – and perhaps even partly because of them – there is much enjoyment in looking over and walking across these battlefields. In doing so, we can try to visualise them at the time of the conflict, working out the positions and strategies of the opposing armies and imagining the scenes of carnage, suffering, brutality, bravery and heroism. Most of the sites are nowadays in peaceful and tranquil surroundings and situated amidst attractive countryside and some of them have features of interest nearby – perhaps a ruined castle, cathedral, ancient house, old church or abbey – to add to the interest and enjoyment of the walk.

The battlefield walks are supplemented by routes featuring some famous sieges and other events of military significance that have occurred in the Midlands. The latter include Charles II's attempts to elude capture after his defeat at Worcester in 1651, Bonnie Prince Charlie's momentous visit to Derby in 1745, and the destruction of most of the centre of Coventry in World War II.

Where relevant, suggestions for possible follow up visits to sites in the locality – not on the actual route – that have a link with the battle have been included. These may be a museum that has displays and exhibits to do with the battle or siege or a memorial in a local church to someone who played a role in the battle. These all help to build up a picture of these stirring, violent but memorable events that took place in the past and have helped to shape the present.

Brian Conduit

Contents

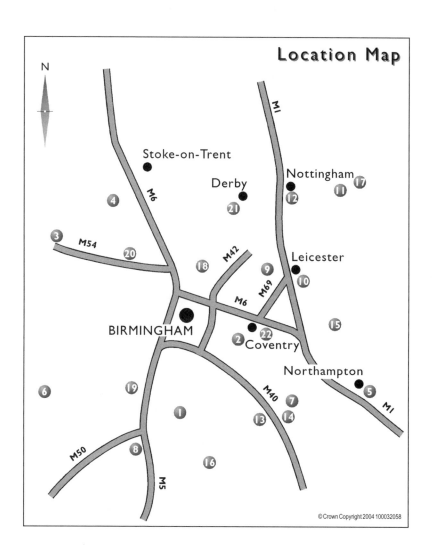

Location Map

N

Stoke-on-Trent

Derby

Nottingham

Leicester

BIRMINGHAM

Coventry

Northampton

M1
M6
4
3 M54
20
18 M42
M69
9
10
15
21
12
11
17
M6
2 22
6
19
1
M40
7
13
14
5
M1
M50
8
M5
16

© Crown Copyright 2004 100032058

Introduction

Significance of the Midlands

The Midlands is the crossroads of England. Crossroads are meeting places for all sorts of activities – personal and family affairs, commerce and also warfare. Throughout England's often turbulent history, it is not surprising that armies have repeatedly clashed in the Midlands as they converged on each other from different parts of the country. In rebellions and civil wars, whichever side controlled the heartland, was well on the way to controlling the whole country.

During the Middle Ages and in Tudor and Stuart times, many cities and towns in the Midlands occupied key strategic positions, possessing powerful castles or controlling vital river crossings and road junctions. Places that immediately spring to mind are Newark, Nottingham, Leicester, Kenilworth, Worcester, Hereford, Ludlow and Shrewsbury. In a more recent conflict, the Second World War, the great Midland industrial cities – Birmingham, Wolverhampton and Coventry – became key targets for enemy bombers, as they were major centres of armaments manufacture.

Of the 22 walks in this guide, 14 take you to specific battlefield sites. These vary considerably and among them are the locations of some of the most decisive and significant battles in our history. The other eight are a miscellany but are all concerned with military conflict. Three are sieges and the remainder either follow in the footsteps of people before or after battles or, in the case of Coventry, look at the evidence of wartime bombing.

The vast majority of the conflicts – involving 17 out of the 22 walks – took place either during or just after the two major civil wars in our history: the Wars of the Roses and the Civil War between King Charles I and Parliament. Therefore it would be useful and help both to make sense of the battles and to put them in perspective if battlefield walkers were aware of what was involved in both these wars and the military ups and downs throughout them. Battles in the Midlands do not make much sense if seen in isolation from significant battles in other parts of the country.

The Wars of the Roses (1455-85)

From the start there are two vital points to understand about the Wars of the Roses. First they have nothing to do with the counties of Lancashire and Yorkshire, and secondly there were no ideological differences between the opposing sides. The wars were purely a struggle for power between the Houses of Lancaster and York and their various supporters. In 1399, Henry, Duke of Lancaster, descendant of Edward III, had overthrown Richard II and become King Henry IV, first of the Lancastrian kings. He was succeeded in turn by Henry V and Henry VI. Henry VI was a weak king and suffered from bouts of insanity and during his reign the country drifted into disorder. From 1453, after defeat by France in the Hundred Years' War, there was an increase in discontent which was spearheaded by Richard, Duke of York, also a descendant of Edward III.

War broke put in 1455 and, following Yorkist victories at Blore Heath and Mortimer's Cross, Henry VI was deposed and the son of Richard, Duke of York – Richard himself was killed at Wakefield in 1460 – became Edward IV, first of the Yorkist kings in 1461. This did not end the wars. As long as the deposed king was alive and had an heir, the Lancastrians continued the struggle, led by Henry's consort, Queen Margaret. In 1470, after Edward's principal ally, Richard Neville, Earl of Warwick – 'Warwick the Kingmaker' – had changed sides, Edward was forced to flee to France and Henry VI was temporarily reinstated but after decisive victories at Barnet and Tewkesbury in 1471, Edward IV was finally safe. Henry's son and heir was killed at Tewkesbury and Henry VI himself was murdered soon afterwards in the Tower of London.

After twelve years of relative stability, the country was plunged into chaos again with the premature death of Edward IV in 1483. His heir – Edward V – was a boy and the throne was seized by his uncle, Richard, Duke of Gloucester, who became King Richard III. In 1485, an invasion by Henry Tudor, heir to the Lancastrian cause, resulted in Richard's defeat and death at Bosworth and the accession of Henry VII. Although there were still uprisings and attempts to seize the throne, the advent of the powerful Tudor dynasty ushered in a more stable era.

The Civil War (1642-49)

If the Wars of the Roses could be said to have ended in the Midlands with the battles of Bosworth and Stoke Field, the next civil war started in the Midlands in 1642 with Charles I's raising of the royal standard at Nottingham. For some years conflict had been brewing between Charles I and Parliament. Like the Wars of the Roses, the Civil War was a struggle for power but this time there was an important principle at stake. Charles believed in the divine right of kings; Parliament in the right of the elected representatives to have a greater say in how the country was governed.

Compromise was out after Charles ruled for eleven years – from 1629 to 1640 – without calling a Parliament. When recalled, Parliament was in an ugly mood. For many of its members the last straw was the attempt by the king to arrest five of them – those who he regarded as the chief troublemakers – in January 1642. It was unsuccessful and throughout the spring and summer of 1642, the country slowly but surely drifted into war as both sides began building up armies. In general, the south and east – including London – were for Parliament and the north and west for the king.

Because of the hostility of London, Charles left his capital and journeyed to the north and the unfurling of the royal standard outside the walls of Nottingham Castle in August 1642 marked the official beginning of the conflict. Initially the king had the more experienced armies and his main aim was to win the war quickly by capturing London. On his march south, he was intercepted at Edgehill and although the result was indecisive, it checked his advance on London and he made Oxford his headquarters for the remainder of the war. Further attempts to take London in 1643 failed but the king still had the stronger army and still retained control of large parts of the country.

An alliance between Parliament and the Scots strengthened Parliament's military power and in 1644 the Royalist army was defeated at Marston Moor in Yorkshire. Reorganisation of the Parliamentary army under Fairfax and Cromwell created a more professional and disciplined fighting force, known as the New Model Army, and in 1645 this army won another decisive victory at Naseby. By this time the king was running out of both money and men and defeat looked inevitable. During the summer of 1646,

3

Parliamentary forces mopped up the remaining Royalist garrisons and Charles finally surrendered to the Scots at Newark From then on he was a prisoner for the rest of his life.

That was just the end of the First Civil War. While in custody, the king made an agreement with the Scots and in 1648 a Scottish army invaded England to start the brief Second Civil War. Cromwell quickly defeated the Scots and, because of the king's treachery, he was put on trial for treason. He was found guilty and executed on 30 January 1649.

Even this was not the end. Charles I's son was crowned Charles II in Scotland and invaded England to claim his throne. But Cromwell inflicted a crushing defeat on him at Worcester in 1651 and Charles was forced to flee into exile. The war was finally over and England became a republic but soon after the death of Cromwell, the monarchy was restored in 1660.

Uncertainties and disagreements

When walking battlefield sites, it is important to be aware that a lot of the information about battles and battlefields is conjectural and open to question and debate. A lack of detailed, accurate and especially unbiased historical evidence means that, in the case of many battles, the interpretation of that evidence is an area of conflict amongst specialist military historians. Therefore disagreements do arise regarding the exact events and the precise disposition of rival armies.

Further reading

A.H. Burne – *The Battlefields of England* (Penguin, 2002)

John Kinross – *Discovering Battlefields of England and Scotland* (Shire, 1998)

David Smurthwaite – *The Complete Guide to the Battlefields of Britain* (Michael Joseph, 1993)

Philip Warner – *British Battlefields: The Midlands* (Osprey, 1973)

Ken and Denise Guest – *British Battles* (Harper Collins, 1996)

1

The Battle of Evesham, 4 August 1265

Evesham is a particularly difficult battle site to see because much of it is covered with houses and the western slopes are on private land and inaccessible. It is here that an obelisk was erected but this cannot be seen from the road. As compensation, the eastern slopes have not been built on, are accessible by public footpaths and give superb views over the Avon valley. The return leg is a beautiful walk by the Avon, passing orchards which look at their best at blossom time.

Start: Evesham, Market Square, grid ref SP037437

Distance: 4½ miles (7.2km)

Time: 2 hours

Parking: Evesham

Refreshments: Pubs and cafés at Evesham

Map: OS Explorer 205 (Stratford-upon-Avon & Evesham)

In 1215, the English barons had forced a reluctant King John to sign Magna Carta, which gave them certain rights and, for the first time, limited the power of the king. This created problems for his successor, the young Henry III, as the barons, having tasted power and success, now wanted a greater role in governing the country. By the middle of the 13th century, some of them, led by Simon de Montfort, Earl of Leicester, were accusing Henry of failing to honour the terms of Magna Carta and discontent was mounting.

What is called the Baron's War broke out in 1264 and Simon de Montfort and his allies decisively defeated Henry and his son, Prince Edward – the future Edward I – at the battle of Lewes. After this victory, de Montfort effectively controlled the government as

The bell tower is virtually all that remains of the medieval Evesham Abbey. In the foreground there is a memorial to Simon de Montfort on the site of his alleged grave at the east end of the abbey church.

Henry III was virtually his puppet and Prince Edward was held as a hostage to the king's good behaviour. Not surprisingly there was still unrest and opposition and it was partly in an attempt to quell this that de Montfort summoned what is often regarded as the first real English Parliament in January 1265.

In May 1265, Prince Edward escaped from custody and forged an alliance with one of de Montfort's chief adversaries, Gilbert de Clare, Earl of Gloucester. As one of the most powerful of the Marcher Lords, Gloucester was angered by de Montfort's attempts to ally with Llewellyn, Prince of Wales. Edward and his army based themselves at Worcester and de Montfort, having made an agreement with Llewellyn to supply him with troops, prepared to march from his base at Hereford to join up with his son – also called Simon – at the family stronghold of Kenilworth Castle. Unknown to him, Edward made a surprise attack on Kenilworth, following a rapid march from Worcester, and killed many of the younger Simon's men.

After his return to Worcester, Edward set out to intercept de Montfort as he continued his march to Kenilworth. On 3 August, de Montfort reached Evesham, where the River Avon does a loop around the town, and camped there. He had walked right into a trap as he was almost certainly unaware that Edward's forces were so close, just to the north of the town and closing in on him. On the next day, Edward advanced on the town. With the advantage of having far greater numbers, Edward split his armies into three to block de Montfort's possible escape routes. Edward and Gloucester occupied the low ridge of Greenhill to the north of Evesham and Roger Mortimer controlled Bengeworth Bridge over the River Avon.

It was only on the morning of 4 August that de Montfort realised his perilous position after sending a look out up onto the central tower of Evesham Abbey. Vastly outnumbered, enclosed within the town and with the river crossings controlled by Edward's forces, he decided that his only hope was to try and force his way through the middle of the enemy lines to the north. But the two wings of the Royalist army converged on his men from the slopes of Greenhill and there was a virtual massacre. To make matters worse, the battle was fought in bad light and a violent thunderstorm. Many of de Montfort's Welsh allies fled from the carnage and tried to escape by swimming across the Avon near Offenham Bridge, where many were either drowned or killed in the adjacent meadow known as Dead Man's Ait. Simon de Montfort himself was killed but Henry III, who had been in the custody of the barons all the time and was dragged by them into the battle, miraculously emerged from it uninjured and was reunited with his victorious son.

The Route

1. Facing the former town hall, turn right along an alley, passing to the right of a 15th-century, timber-framed house. Cross Bridge Street, keep ahead under an arch and continue along Evesham's broad High Street. This is roughly the route taken by Simon de Montfort and his army to the battle. After crossing a railway bridge, the road ascends Greenhill – the site of the battle.

2. On the brow of the hill, turn right, at a public footpath sign, along an enclosed path. Soon come views over the Avon valley from the eastern slopes of the hill. At a waymarked post, turn left to walk along the top edge of sloping orchards and fields. In the corner of a field, follow the path first to the right and then to the left, go through a hedge gap and continue along the top edge of the next field to a T-junction. The main route continues to the right but,

for a brief detour to the site of the Battle Well, turn left along a tarmac track to a road, cross over and walk along The Squires as far as a hedge gap on the left.

3. Although there is no access and nothing to see, a shallow depression in the field in front is the site of the Battle Well, where it is alleged Simon de Montfort was killed. In later years, it became a centre for pilgrimages as it was believed to have curative powers and a small chapel may have been erected over it. There is no trace of this. Retrace your steps to the tarmac track (Blayneys Lane) and continue downhill along it. Where it bends right, keep ahead along a hedge-lined track, which narrows to a path and reaches a stile. Turn right over it and walk along the left edge of a field, parallel to the Evesham bypass, to a tarmac track. Turn left over a stile and cross the busy main road carefully. Climb a stile, keep ahead along a tarmac track but after about 100 yards (91m), turn right through a kissing gate and head across meadows to the banks of the River Avon opposite the pub at Offenham.

4. At the time of the battle there was a bridge here and later a ferry. Now there are neither. The adjoining meadows, Dead Man's Ait, were the scene of great carnage in 1265 as many of de Montfort's Welsh allies were killed by the enemy or drowned while desperately trying to escape by swimming across the river. Turn right beside the river and pass under the bypass. Keep ahead, climbing a stile, and, at the end of the meadow, go through a kissing gate and continue through a belt of trees. Go under a railway bridge and the riverside path later widens into a track. At a fork by a footpath post, take the left-hand enclosed path, go through a kissing gate and keep ahead along a tarmac path, which bears right away from the river to a road.

5. Turn left and, at a junction, bear left along Mill Street to a T-junction just to the right of Bengeworth Bridge. This is a modern successor of the bridge held by Roger Mortimer to block one of Simon de Montfort's escape routes. Cross over Bridge Street and keep ahead along a paved path into Abbey Park. Immediately turn right and head up to the Bell Tower and the site of de Montfort's tomb. The detached, early 16th-century Bell Tower is virtually all that is left of the once powerful Evesham Abbey and

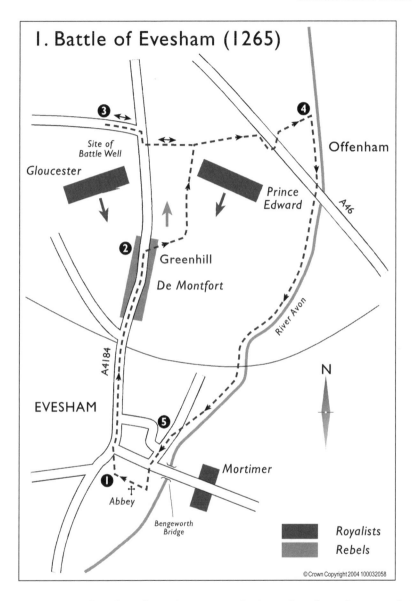

1. Battle of Evesham (1265)

Offenham

Site of Battle Well

Gloucester

Prince Edward

A46

Greenhill

De Montfort

River Avon

A4184

N

EVESHAM

Mortimer

Abbey

Bengeworth Bridge

| | Royalists |
| | Rebels |

© Crown Copyright 2004 100032058

was completed only a few years before the dissolution of the monasteries. Beside it is the memorial to Simon de Montfort on the supposed site of his tomb at the east end of the abbey church. It is believed that Henry III worshipped in the abbey just prior to being taken by de Montfort's forces to the battle. Go under the Bell Tower and the path bends right between the two churches – All Saints and St Lawrence's – to pass under Abbey Gateway into the Market Square.

What else is there to see?

There are displays on the battle in the Simon de Montfort Room in the Almonry Museum at Evesham.

2

The Siege of Kenilworth, 1266

Kenilworth's imposing castle was the target of the six-month siege in 1266 and is inevitably the focal point of this walk. The castle is in sight for much of the way and apart from a brief opening stretch through Abbey Fields to the east, most of the route is across the open and gently undulating countryside to the west of it.

Start: Kenilworth, Castle Green, grid ref SP279724

Distance: 7 miles (11.3km)

Time: 3½ hours

Parking: Kenilworth

Refreshments: Pubs and cafes at Kenilworth, café at Kenilworth Castle

Map: OS Explorer 221 (Coventry & Warwick)

After Simon de Montfort's defeat and death at the Battle of Evesham in August 1265, Henry III and his son Edward needed to subdue and capture the de Montfort stronghold at Kenilworth Castle, occupied by his son, also called Simon. Some of Simon's men, frustrated by the events at Evesham, took it out on the local people and for several months terrorised the countryside around Kenilworth. Meanwhile the king had to deal with problems elsewhere.

In December 1265, Simon went to Lincolnshire and Cambridgeshire to drum up support among his followers but the king followed him and forced his surrender. At Northampton, Simon and Henry made an agreement. Simon was to surrender Kenilworth and leave England in return for a pension.

The garrison at Kenilworth refused these terms, claiming that the castle belonged to Eleanor, the widow of Simon de Montfort – she was also the king's sister – and continued to occupy it. In March 1266, Henry offered generous terms to the leaders of the garrison but they were rejected and in an act of provocation, the king's envoy was sent back minus a hand. Military action now seemed the only option. The king's army set up camp on what is now Castle Green and prepared for a siege. Further provocation came after the Archbishop of Canterbury excommunicated the members of the garrison. Their response was to send the castle surgeon onto the battlements, dressed in clerical robes, where he issued an insulting 'counter-excommunication' of the king, archbishop and their supporters.

The siege began on 21 June. Siege engines arrived from Nottingham and as the castle was almost surrounded by water, boats were transported overland from Chester in order to mount an attack across the Great Mere. A tall mobile tower, nicknamed 'The Bear', was built to enable Henry's archers to fire on the defenders more effectively but they were beaten off by catapults. All attempts to enter the castle and force the defenders to submit failed and therefore the king fell back on negotiation again.

Further lenient terms – known as the Dictum of Kenilworth – were offered to the besieged and again they were rejected. Henry III now prepared to call up extra men, possibly intending to end the resistance by storming the castle. Such action was not necessary as just before Christmas the garrison surrendered, not from military action but – as often in medieval sieges – through an outbreak of disease. The siege had lasted approximately 6 months.

The defenders were allowed to leave with their horses and weapons. The king later bestowed Kenilworth on Edmund, his second son, who was created Earl of Lancaster.

The Route

1. The red sandstone walls and towers of Kenilworth Castle make an impressive sight and must have looked even more formidable when surrounded on three sides by water. A huge lake, the Great Mere, was constructed because the castle lacked the usual natural defence of a hilltop position. Its remains belong to three main periods: the mighty 12th-century keep, John of Gaunt's 14th-century banqueting hall and Leicester's gatehouse, built by

Kenilworth's imposing castle, target of the six-month siege in 1266

Robert Dudley, Earl of Leicester and favourite of Elizabeth I, in the 16th century.

With your back to the castle and facing the green, turn right. At a fork, take the left hand road (Castle Hill) and just after passing Malthouse Lane on the left, bear right onto a tarmac path which heads downhill across Abbey Fields to the scanty remains of Kenilworth Abbey.

2. The ruins mostly comprise a vaulted gatehouse. Although not directly involved in the siege, the monks were impoverished both by the requirement to provide food for the royal army during the long siege and by the later levying of taxes. The path bends right and just beyond the ruins, turn right and keep the swimming baths on your left to reach the end of a pool. Turn right onto a path, between the pool on your right and Finham Brook on your left, to a road. Turn left to cross a footbridge over the brook and turn right along a tarmac drive to Kenilworth Castle car park. To the right is a causeway to the castle and, just beyond it, turn right off the drive to a waymarked kissing gate.

3. The next part of the walk is along the edge of what was the Great Mere. It was not until the middle of the 17th century – after the

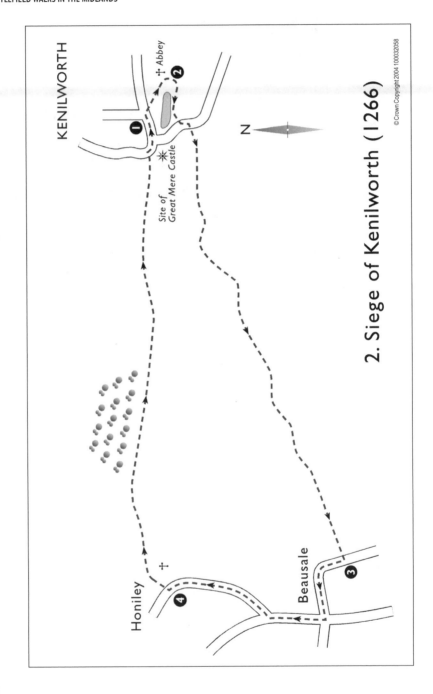

2. Siege of Kenilworth (1266)

KENILWORTH

† Abbey

Site of
Great Mere Castle

N

Honiley

Beausale

© Crown Copyright 2004 100032058

Civil War – that the lake was drained and the land turned over to pasture. After going through the kissing gate, walk along the left edge of a field, go through another kissing gate and in the next field is an upturned boat. This marks the place where people sat to watch a later and rather more peaceful event than the siege – a spectacular fireworks display organised by Robert Dudley for Elizabeth I in 1575.

At the far end of the field, go through a kissing gate. Keep ahead along the left edge of the next two fields and, in the corner of the last one, turn left to climb a stile. Continue across the middle of a succession of fields, climbing a series of stiles, and in the corner of the last field – the route is well-waymarked – go through a hedge gap and turn left to keep along the left edge of the next two fields. In the corner of the second field, turn right to continue along the left edge and look out for where you turn left over a stile. Once more continue across a series of fields and over a succession of stiles, finally walking along an enclosed track to a lane.

4. Turn right, follow the lane around a left bend to a crossroads in the hamlet of Beausale and turn right. Take the first lane on the right, signposted to Honiley. Just after a left bend by Honiley Hall and the 18th-century church, turn right over a stile, at a public footpath sign to Castle. Head across a field to a stile, climb it, walk along a right field edge and look out for where you turn right over a stile to continue along the right edge of the next field.

The curving field edge leads to a footbridge over a brook. Cross it and keep along the left edge of a series of fields until after climbing a stile, the route continues along the right edge of a field. Climb a stile in the corner and follow a worn path, which bears slightly left across the next field. Earthworks in this field indicate that it was the site of The Pleasance, a 15th-century royal pleasure palace situated in the middle of the lake.

The path bears right to a kissing gate in the field corner. Go through and walk along an enclosed path which emerges onto a track. Continue along it – enjoying superb views of the castle – to a road opposite Castle Green and turn right to the start. The attractive Tudor cottages on Castle Green stand on the site of the royal camp in 1266 from where siege engines hurled missiles at the castle walls.

3

Battle of Shrewsbury, 21 July 1403

The site of the battle is to the north of the town, close to industrial estates and main roads and bisected by a railway line. From the wooded slopes of Haughmond Hill, which overlook the battlefield, the route passes by the substantial remains of Haughmond Abbey and then continues across fields to Battlefield church, which stands on the battle site. The return leg takes a slightly different route. There are fine and wide views throughout over Shrewsbury and the surrounding countryside.

Start: Haughmond Hill, Forestry Commission car park, off B5062 to the east of Shrewsbury, grid ref SJ546147

Distance: 7½ miles (12.1km)

Time: 3½ hours

Parking: Haughmond Hill

Refreshments: None

Map: OS Explorer 241(Shrewsbury)

In 1399 Henry Bolingbroke, Duke of Lancaster, seized the throne from Richard II and was crowned Henry IV, the first of the Lancastrian kings. Given the circumstances of his accession, it is hardly surprising that he was faced with widespread opposition and constant rebellions in the early part of his reign. As well as the powerful and troublesome English barons, there was a serious uprising in Wales led by Owen Glyndwr and the maintenance of peace and security on the Scottish borders was a permanent problem. For the security of the Scottish borders, Henry relied on one of his principal supporters, Sir Henry Percy, Earl of Northumberland, and his son Hotspur, but a quarrel developed between the Percies

Haughmond Abbey: the royal army camped near here, prior to the battle of Shrewsbury

and the king over their financial compensation for defending northern England. This resulted in the Percies deserting Henry and joining the ranks of the rebels.

The Percies planned to link up with Owen Glyndwr and marched on Chester. The king moved to Lichfield, where he appears to have learnt that Hotspur was advancing on Shrewsbury where the king's son, Prince Hal, the future Henry V, was commanding a small garrison. Henry marched rapidly to Shrewsbury in order to reinforce his son before the rebels reached there. Both Henry IV and Hotspur arrived on 20 July. The royal army camped on Haughmond Hill near the abbey and Hotspur was a few miles to the west near the banks of the River Severn.

Despite last-ditch attempts by the abbots of Shrewsbury and Haughmond to mediate in the dispute, the armies engaged in battle on the following day on a site about 2 miles (3.2km) to the north of Shrewsbury. Hotspur was outnumbered by the royal troops and was cut off from his allies: his father was still to the north and Glyndwr was in Wales. The rebels occupied a low ridge to the north of the royal army and attacked furiously, hoping to kill the king. There was

3. Battle of Shrewsbury (1403)

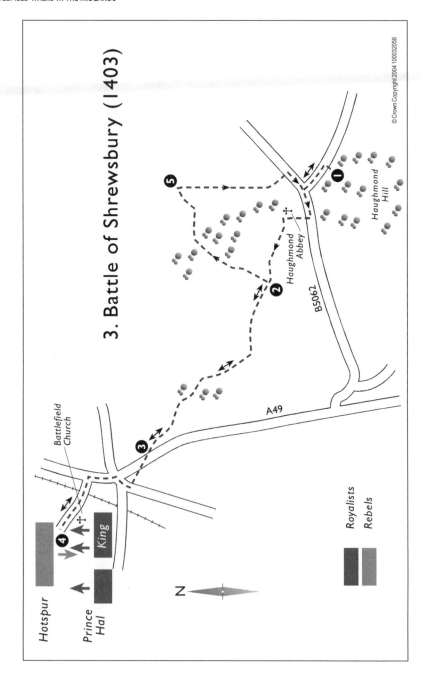

© Crown Copyright 2004 100032058

much fierce and prolonged fighting but the charge was held and eventually a counter-attack, led by a wounded Prince Hal, was successful. Hotspur was killed by an arrow and the defeated rebel army was pursued for several miles.

Battlefield church is the major landmark on the battle site. Hotspur's army occupied the slight ridge to the north of the church and the king's army was to the south.

The Route

1. The starting point on Haughmond Hill was where the royal army camped prior to the battle. Leave the car park; turn left along the road to a T-junction and turn left again, in the Shrewsbury direction, along the B5062. At a sign to Haughmond Abbey, turn right along a track and, in front of the abbey wall, turn left to a stile. Climb it, turn right along the right edge of a field, climb a stile and keep along the right edge of the next field, passing in front of the abbey ruins. The Augustinian abbey of Haughmond was founded in 1135 and dissolved on the orders of Henry VIII in 1539. Little survives of the church but there are substantial remains of the domestic buildings around the cloister, mostly dating from the 13th and 14th centuries.

   After climbing the next stile, turn left along the left edge of a field, go through a gate and keep ahead to a stile. Turn right over it and as you walk diagonally across a field, the church towers and spires of Shrewsbury can be seen on the horizon. Climb a stile, keep in the same direction across the next field, climb another stile and walk along the right field edge to the corner.

2. Keep ahead over a footbridge and make for the far right corner of the next field where you cross a brook. Go through a gate and keep ahead along a track which curves slightly left towards a farm. Go through a gate to a crossways in front of the farm buildings and turn right along a track. Look for where you turn left over a stile, walk diagonally across a field and in the far corner, climb a stile onto a tarmac track. Turn left and, where the track bends right, keep ahead through a gate and continue along an enclosed track, which descends through woodland. At a fork and fingerpost just after crossing a bridge over a brook, take the right-hand

track, which heads up to a stile on the edge of the trees. Climb it, continue uphill across a field, making for the corner of a wall by a large house, bear right alongside the wall and climb a stile. Keep ahead along a track, turn left over a stile, walk across the corner of a field and climb another stile. Turn left along a wide, enclosed track but almost immediately, turn right through a gap between twin trunks of the same tree, climb a stile and keep along the left edge of the next two fields – there are more stiles – finally emerging onto the A49.

3. Cross this busy road carefully, climb a stile opposite and turn right along the right edge of a field. After about 100 yards (91m) – at a footpath post – bear left across the field and go through a gate on the far side roughly equidistant between the two corners. Keep ahead to a road, turn right to a traffic island, turn left, cross Battlefield Link Road and keep ahead along a path beside the A49. At a sign for Battlefield Church, turn left along a narrow lane, pass under a railway bridge and keep ahead to the church, turning left through a car park into the churchyard.

Henry IV founded the church in 1408 as a chantry chapel in memory of those killed in the battle and some of the gargoyles are supposed to be representations of some of the rebel forces. It stands on the battle site but whether it is situated in the centre of the battlefield is open to doubt. As you face the church from the north, the royal army was based in the fields in front and Hotspur's men occupied the slight ridge behind you.

4. Retrace your steps to point 2 and after crossing the footbridge, turn left along the left edge of a field. Climb a stile in the corner, keep ahead to climb another one and continue gently uphill along the right edge of a field, by the woodland of New Coppice on the right. At the top, climb a stile, keep ahead through a kissing gate, bear right and walk diagonally across a field. In the far corner, turn left through another kissing gate. Keep by the right field edge, which curves right and turn right through a kissing gate.

5. Walk along an enclosed track which curves left, passing to the right of Haughmond Farm, to a road. Turn right and take the first road on the left, signposted to Upton Magna and Withington, to return to the start.

What else is there to see?

There is a heritage site with information boards, and a short battle-field trail, signposted from the A49 to the north of Shrewsbury.

4

The Battle of Blore Heath, 23 September 1459

The battlefield lies across the present A53 between Loggerheads and Market Drayton. There is a memorial cross in a field opposite Audley's Cross Farm but this is inaccessible and difficult to see from the road. The route uses lanes and public rights of way that encircle the approximate site of the battle and from these there are extensive views over it.

Start: The drive to Bloreheath Farm, on the A53 about half-way between Loggerheads and Market Drayton, grid ref SJ708354

Distance: 3 miles (4.8km)

Time: 1½ hours

Parking: One of the two lay-bys on the A53 either side of the drive to Bloreheath Farm

Refreshments: None

Map: OS Explorer 243 (Market Drayton)

The opening battle of the Wars of the Roses, at St Albans in 1455, was a decisive Yorkist victory. The Lancastrian king, Henry VI, continued on the throne but Richard, Duke of York, and his supporters, including the powerful Neville family, were given positions of influence within the government. For the next four years, there was a rather uneasy and fragile peace during which both sides raised armies, kept a close watch on each other and constantly tried to manoeuvre into advantageous positions.

In particular, Queen Margaret, Henry VI's ambitious and resourceful consort, attempted to build up support, gather recruits for the Lancastrian cause and generally reduce the power of York and the Nevilles. By 1459 further conflict was inevitable.

At the time, the Yorkists were at a disadvantage as their armies were scattered. Richard, Duke of York, was raising troops on the Welsh Borders, Richard Neville, Earl of Warwick, was in Calais and his father, Lord Salisbury, was in Yorkshire. Salisbury planned to join forces with York at Ludlow Castle and from there the combined armies would march on London.

Henry VI and Margaret were at Eccleshall in Staffordshire and Margaret sent a force of around 10,000 under Lord Audley to intercept and arrest Salisbury before he could join up with York. The rival armies took up position on either side of a small stream, Hempmill Brook, at Blore Heath near Market Drayton. Audley and the Lancastrians occupied a strong defensive position on a low ridge, on the west side of the brook. Salisbury was on the eastern side and used a clever strategy. He hid part of his army behind slopes and tricked Audley into a frontal assault, possibly by pretending to retreat. Audley charged across the brook, but his troops were cut down by the Yorkist archers and infantry. There was much savage

The Yorkist and Lancastrian armies were deployed on either side of the Hempmill Brook during the Battle of Blore Heath.

fighting and the Lancastrians were beaten back. After Audley was killed, the Lancastrians fled along the bed of the brook, pursued by the victorious enemy, and many tried to escape by crossing the River Tern at its confluence with the brook. It was a convincing Yorkist victory.

The Route

1. A plaque at the entrance to Bloreheath Farm indicates that the farm was near the site of the Lancastrian camp. With your back to the farm entrance, turn right along the A53 to the first crossroads and turn left along a lane signposted to Mucklestone and Knighton. The crossroads was in the thick of the fighting and Hempmill Brook, the dividing line between the rival armies, flows under the main road here.

2. Just before reaching a T-junction, turn right through a gate, at a public footpath sign, and walk along the left edge of a field. After going through another gate, the route continues along the right inside edge of woodland and, at a public footpath sign, turns left through the trees to a track. Turn right, head gently uphill through woodland, climb a stile and keep ahead to the A53.

3. Cross over to a public footpath sign and follow a path diagonally across a field to a stile on the far side. Climb it, cross the tarmac drive to Blore Farm, climb the stile opposite and continue in the same direction across the next field to a stile. After climbing that one, descend a bank to ford Hempmill Brook – strategically placed planks aid the crossing – and climb another stile. The brook was probably wider in 1459 than it is now but the fairly steep embankments on the eastern side indicate that any assault across it would have been difficult. Head uphill across a field and, in the corner, climb a stile onto a lane.

4. Turn right and, at a T-junction, keep ahead over a stile – there is a public footpath sign here – and walk along the left edge of a field. Climb a stile, turn right along a short section of enclosed path, climb another stile and turn left along the left edge of a field. Continue along a track and in the field corner, turn right to keep by the field edge – still along a track – to the A53 again. Turn left to return to the start.

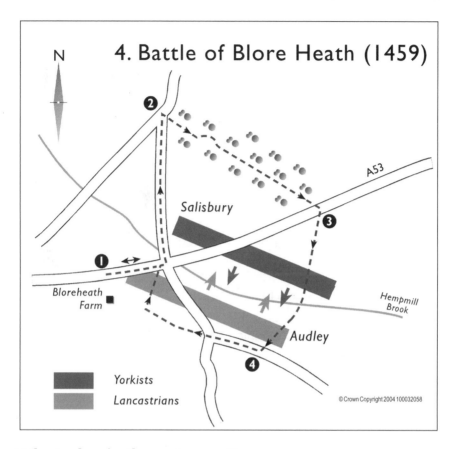

What else is there to see?

Opposite the church in the village of Mucklestone, about 1½ miles (2.4km) to the north-east, there is a plaque on the wall of a house, facing an anvil that was erected in the churchyard. It records that Queen Margaret had the shoes on her horse reversed by the local blacksmith in order to get away quickly after the defeat of her army.

5

The Battle of Northampton, 10 July 1460

Much of the battlefield is covered by suburban housing, busy roads and industrial estates on the southern outskirts of Northampton. But some meadowland survives beside the River Nene and parallel Grand Union Canal, plus a large area of parkland – much of it now a golf course – around Delapre Abbey. The route starts from the site of the Yorkist camp on Hunsbury Hill, descends to the River Nene and continues along the river before heading back through Delapre Park.

Start: Hunsbury Hill Country Park, about 2 miles (3.2km) to the south west of Northampton town centre, grid ref SP735585

Distance: 7½ miles (12.1km)

Time: 3½ hours

Parking: Hunsbury Hill Country Park

Refreshments: None

Map: OS Explorer 207 (Newport Pagnell & Northampton South) or 223 (Northampton & Market Harborough)

In July 1460, a Yorkist army occupied London and then continued northwards. Henry VI and his queen, Margaret – plus the Duke of Buckingham – moved southwards from Coventry and set up camp beside the River Nene on the southern outskirts of Northampton. They had a well-defended position but were outnumbered by their Yorkist opponents.

Edward, the son of Richard Duke of York – the future Edward IV – and Richard Neville, Earl of Warwick, led the Yorkist army. On the night before the battle it camped on Hunsbury Hill, the site of an

The nedieval predecessor to the present mansion of Delapre Abbey overlooked the site of the Battle of Northampton

Iron Age fort which overlooks the Nene valley and the Lancastrian position. Before daylight, Edward and Warwick descended from their hilltop position and attacked the Lancastrians across the marshes near Delapre Abbey. Two spectators who watched the battle from the nearby Eleanor Cross were the Archbishop of Canterbury and a legate from the Pope.

Conditions were terrible. Despite being in the middle of the summer, it poured with rain all day and the mud slowed down the Yorkist advance and potentially made their forces sitting targets for the Lancastrian bowmen. But the Yorkists received an unexpected and welcome bonus, which enabled them to turn the tables. Lord Grey of Ruthin, a cousin of the queen, appears to have struck a deal with Warwick and told his men to lay down their arms. Lancastrian resistance crumbled and they fled from the battlefield. Many were drowned while trying to swim across the swollen river.

Buckingham was amongst those killed and Henry VI became a prisoner. Richard, Duke of York, returned to England from Ireland to claim the throne and a compromise was reached whereby Henry remained as king but Richard was given the title of Protector and made the heir to the throne. Thus Henry's son, Edward Prince of Wales, was bypassed and robbed of his inheritance, a situation totally unacceptable to his mother, the resourceful Queen Margaret. The Wars of the Roses continued.

The Route

1. Begin by taking the path that leads off from the corner of the car park into woodland and bear left on joining another path. Head gently uphill through the trees and after about 200 yards (183m), turn left onto another path. There is no waymark here and the only landmarks are a dog litter bin and another path leading off to the right a few yards ahead. The path keeps along the outer defences of the tree-covered Iron Age fort to the right, 371 feet (113m) high.

   Where the path emerges into open country, keep ahead across grass, by a fence on the left, and ahead are fine views across the Nene valley and Northampton. It was on these heights that the Yorkist army camped on the night before the battle and from where it launched its attack on the outnumbered Lancastrians, entrenched below in the meadows on the south side of the River Nene. Turn left at a T-junction and on joining a tarmac track, bear left to the end of a road by school buildings.

2. Keep ahead and the road curves right to a roundabout. Turn right to another roundabout on the A45, cross carefully and keep ahead downhill along Hunsbury Hill Avenue. Where the road bends left, keep ahead along an enclosed track which crosses, in succession, four bridges – the first over a disused railway, the second and third over arms of the Grand Union Canal and the fourth over meadowland.

3. Just beyond the last bridge, turn right along a path, at a Nene Valley Way sign, bear slightly right along the right edge of a car park and continue between a lake on the right and the River Nene on the left. The path curves right around the end of the lake and, at a fork, take the right-hand path. Turn left at a footpath post, in the St James Mill Road direction, and turn left again at a T-junction. At the next one, turn right and cross a footbridge over the canal. Go through a kissing gate, keep ahead to a crossways and

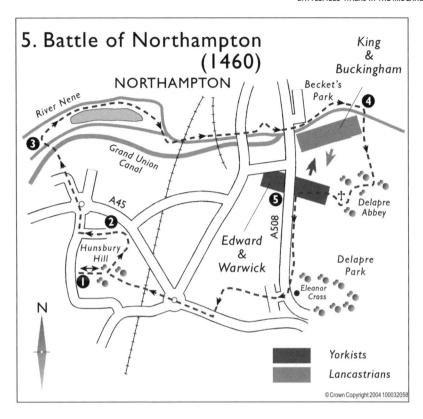

5. Battle of Northampton (1460)

turn left towards a railway viaduct. Turn left over the next foot-bridge and, at a T-junction, turn right beside the River Nene again.

Pass under the viaduct, keep ahead to go under the arch of a railway bridge, continue beside the river and the path rises to a fork. Take the left hand path which keeps beside a road, cross the busy A43, turn right along a tarmac track and turn left at footpath and cycleway signs to Town Centre. The tarmac track bends left away from the river beside a channel. Turn right to cross a footbridge and, at a T-junction in front of a brewery, turn right and the path bends left to continue beside the Nene.

Cross the A508 and on the corner of Cattle Market Road, turn right beside a toilet block and continue along a riverside path. After passing a lock, the path continues through Beckets Park.

The factories and new apartment blocks on the other side of the river occupy part of the battle site.

4. Just before the path emerges into a car park, turn right, at a public footpath sign to Hardingstone, along a road, crossing two bridges over channels of the Nene. Keep ahead along an enclosed tarmac track, passing to the left of the Avon Cosmetics factory. Where the track ends, keep ahead along a path which crosses a disused railway line and passes to the left of marshalling yards and factories to emerge onto the end of a road.

Turn left along a track and, at a T-junction, turn right and cross a footbridge over a brook. To the left is a lake. Walk along an enclosed path, here leaving the rather untidy, semi-industrial area to enter the greener and more attractive surroundings of Delapre Park. At a crossways, turn right along a tree-lined path. Keep ahead on joining a track and, at a wall corner, turn left beside a gate. Almost immediately turn right onto a path which winds through woodland and parkland and finally bends right alongside Delapre Abbey.

The battle was fought in the riverside meadows close to the medieval abbey. After the dissolution of the monasteries by Henry VIII in the 16th century, a large house was built on the site. The present building mainly dates from the 17th and 19th centuries. Turn right to pass in front of the house and continue along a tarmac drive towards a road.

5. On reaching it, turn left – not along the pavement but along a parallel path through trees between the road and the park. Soon after entering Delapre Wood, look out for a path on the right, which emerges onto the road at the end of a wall. Turn left to the Eleanor Cross, one of three surviving crosses from the original twelve. They were built by Edward I to mark the resting-places of his wife's funeral cortege on its journey from Nottinghamshire – where Queen Eleanor died in 1290 – to London. From here it is alleged that the Archbishop of Canterbury and a Papal Legate watched the battle.

Just beyond the cross, turn right into Parkfield Avenue, turn right at a T-junction and turn left into Glastonbury Road. Where it bends left, keep ahead along an enclosed path to the right of a school entrance and just before reaching a barrier, bear right along another enclosed path. Follow it around several bends, keeping the school fence on your left all the while, turn left at a T-junction – still by the school fence – and the path bends right and left to emerge onto the A45. Turn right along a tree-lined footpath with a cycleway beside it.

Go under a road bridge, turn right at a T-junction to pass under another bridge and turn left to go under a third one. The tarmac track heads gently uphill and, where it curves slightly left, turn right onto a path to re-enter Hunsbury Hill Country Park. The path ascends gently, keeps to the left of the Iron Age fort and leads back to the start.

6

The Battle of Mortimer's Cross, 2 February 1461

This is largely quiet and unspoilt countryside and Mortimer's Cross has changed less than most battlefields over the last five and a half centuries. The walk encircles the site and from several points, there are extensive views across it. It also passes a monument to the battle, situated in front of the Monument Inn.

Start: Kingsland, by church and village green, grid ref SO447615

Distance: 6½ miles (10.5km)

Time: 3½ hours

Parking: Roadside parking at Kingsland

Refreshments: Pubs and café at Kingsland, pub at Mortimer's Cross

Map: OS Explorer 203 (Ludlow)

The Yorkist cause suffered a serious blow when Richard, Duke of York was defeated and killed at the Battle of Wakefield in December 1460. His successor, the 18-year old Edward, Earl of March – the future Edward IV – was at Gloucester and marched north to avenge his father's death. At the same time a Lancastrian army, comprising mainly Welsh and Irish soldiers, landed in Wales and marched towards Leominster. It was led by Jasper Tudor, Earl of Pembroke, and the Earl of Ormonde. Their aims were to capture Edward and to prevent him joining up with his powerful ally, the Earl of Warwick.

The encounter between the two armies took place in the

meadows beside the River Lugg that stretched from the road junction of Mortimer's Cross southwards towards the village of Kingsland. The river formed the eastern boundary of the battle site. The Yorkists, who greatly outnumbered the Lancastrian force, were drawn up to the west of the river, facing the enemy who were roughly to the west of the present A4110. A local landowner and Yorkist supporter, Sir Richard Croft, took part in the battle and, using his knowledge of local conditions, advised Edward to let the Lancastrians attack first.

The vanguard of the Lancastrian forces won its initial assault and chased the Yorkists off the field but when it returned, the rest of the army had all but been defeated and were being forced into the village of Kingsland. Yorkist losses were light but the Lancastrians lost over 3,000 men. Both Pembroke and Ormonde escaped but Pembroke's father, Owen Tudor, was captured and executed on the following day at Hereford.

As the words on the battle monument (shown right) say: "... this was the decisive battle which fixed Edward IV on the throne of England".

Despite a Lancastrian victory in the second

This monument to the Battle of Mortimer's Cross stands in front of an inn

Battle of St Albans a few weeks later, Edward, Duke of York, was proclaimed King Edward IV at the beginning of March.

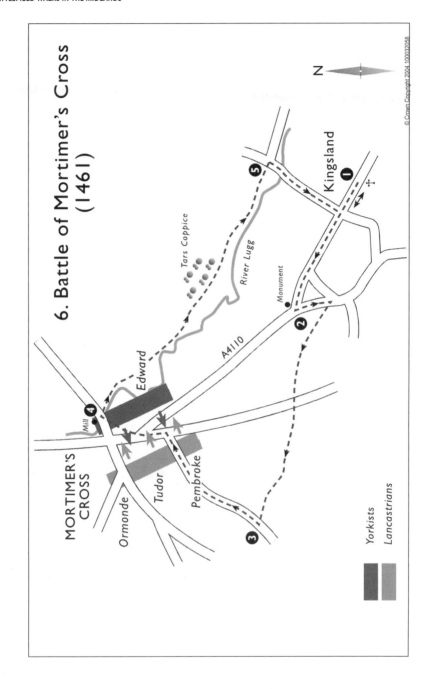

6. Battle of Mortimer's Cross (1461)

The Route

1. Kingsland church overlooks the village green and was built mainly between 1290 and 1310. The Volka chapel, which opens off the north porch, is thought to have been built as a chantry chapel for those killed in the battle. With your back to the church, turn left along the road through the village and after three-quarters of a mile (1.2km), you reach a T-junction by the Monument Inn. In front of the inn is the monument to the battle, erected in 1799.

2. Turn left – be careful as this is a busy road and initially there is no verge – and turn right over a stile beside the gate to Broadleaf Farm. Bear left across the corner of the field to climb another stile and turn right along an enclosed track. Go through a gate, walk along the right edge of a field, climb a stile and keep ahead across a sports field to go through another gate. Continue along the right edge of the next two fields, climb a stile in the corner of the last field, keep ahead to climb another one, continue across the next field and climb a stile onto a lane. Climb the stile opposite, bear right across to the next stile, climb that one and walk along the left edge of an orchard. Continue in a straight line across orchards and after climbing two stiles in quick succession, turn right along the right edge of the next orchard to a waymarked post. Turn left, head across to a T-junction, keep ahead over an area of scrub to the corner of a hut and continue along a track. Keep ahead between huts, climb an embankment, walk along the left edge of an orchard and go through a gate onto a lane in front of a half-timbered house.

3. Turn right along this narrow lane and after a right-hand bend, there is a fine panoramic view across the whole of the battle site. Turn left at a T-junction and, at the next one, cross the road to a stile. Climb it bear left across a field and on the far side, climb another stile onto a road. The crossroads called Mortimer's Cross, from which the battle gets its name, is just to the left and some of the heaviest fighting took place in the vicinity. Turn right, cross the bridge over the River Lugg and to the left is Mortimer's Cross (or Lucton) Mill, an 18th-century water mill still in working order.

Inside, there is a small exhibition about the battle but there are restricted opening times.

4. Immediately after crossing the bridge, turn right over a stile, head across the river and keep along or above its bank to the far tapering end of a field. Turn sharp left here – by a hedge on the right – turn right through a waymarked gate and turn right again (doubling back) along the right edge of a field. In the corner cross a footbridge over a brook, go through a gate, keep ahead across the next field and go through another gate on the far side. Walk along an enclosed path by the river again, keep ahead to climb a stile, bear left uphill across the next field and on the brow, look out for where you go through a gap. Walk straight across the next field to a waymarked stile, climb it and continue by the right edge of woodland (Tars Coppice). At a waymarked post, bear right downhill across the field, go through a gate in the bottom corner and continue beside the Lugg again. The river formed the eastern boundary of the battlefield. After going through a gate, the path bends left to a waymarked post where you turn right first through an area of scrub and young trees and then by the river. Bear left away from the field edge to a stile, climb it, keep ahead across the field corner and climb a stile by the corner of a building. Walk along an enclosed path, go through a gate and keep ahead along a track to a road.

5. Turn right, cross a bridge over the Lugg and follow the road into Kingsland. At a T-junction, turn left to return to the start.

What else is there to see?

The tomb of Sir Richard Croft is in the tiny Croft church adjacent to Croft Castle. The castle is just off the B4362 about 2 miles (3.2km) to the east of Mortimer's Cross. Sir Richard lived until 1507 and became an impressive battle veteran, surviving the battles of Tewkesbury and Stoke Field as well as Mortimer's Cross.

7

The Battle of Edgcote, 26 July 1469

The battle was fought on Danes Moor, an attractive, undulating area which rises to around 560 feet (170m) on the Northamptonshire-Oxfordshire border. Much of the battlefield is virtually unaltered and is surrounded and crossed by lanes and public footpaths. The walk starts in the village of Chipping Warden, passes through the hamlet from which the battle takes its name and goes across the heart of the site.

Start: Chipping Warden, crossroads in village centre, grid ref SP499488

Distance: 6 miles (9.7km)

Time: 3 hours

Parking: Roadside parking at Chipping Warden

Refreshments: Pubs at Chipping Warden

Map: OS Explorer 206 (Edge Hill & Fenny Compton)

By the late 1460s, Edward IV's main difficulties were not with his defeated Lancastrian opponents but with his powerful ally, Richard Neville, Earl of Warwick. Disagreements arose mainly over the rise of the Woodville family at court, following the king's marriage to Elizabeth Woodville in 1464, and the conduct of foreign policy: Warwick favoured an alliance with the King of France while Edward championed the French king's rival, the Duke of Burgundy. The rift between Edward and the Earl of Warwick led to Warwick changing sides and giving his support to the Lancastrians; hence his nickname 'Warwick the Kingmaker'. He went off to Calais with the king's disaffected brother, the unreliable Duke of Clarence, and there the pair waited for an opportunity to return.

The opportunity was provided by a rather shadowy and

Edgcote church and the adjacent great house were close to the Civil War conflict of Edgcote in 1469

unknown figure called Robin of Redesdale. In 1469 he launched a rebellion in the north against the king and headed south in support of the Lancastrian cause. Edward marched north to Nottingham to deal with the uprising but Redesdale slipped past him and continued southwards towards London. Meanwhile Warwick and Clarence returned to England, landed in Kent and moved on to London. In return, the king sent for reinforcements from his allies, the Earls of Pembroke and Devon, who set off from Wales to join him.

On 25 July, the day before the battle, a quarrel seems to have broken out at Banbury between Pembroke and Devon over billeting arrangements and the latter withdrew his men, thus weakening the Yorkist forces. Pembroke continued through the Midlands and camped on low ground on Danes Moor near Edgcote, between Banbury and Daventry, unaware that the enemy was close by. On the morning of 26 July, he found himself almost surrounded on three sides by Lancastrian forces, which occupied the enclosing hills. Although outnumbered, Pembroke attacked with great vigour and courage and managed to take two of the three hills – including the hill occupied by Edgcote Lodge Farm – but with heavy losses. While storming the third hill, the enemy was reinforced by an unruly mob of irregular soldiers from Northampton, gathered together by Sir John Clapham, a Lancastrian supporter. This decided the outcome. The Yorkists were decisively defeated and many of the Welsh troops fled across the River Cherwell at Trafford Bridge and continued northwards along the road now known as Welsh Road. Pembroke was captured and he and his brother were executed at Banbury the next day. Devon's non-participation in the conflict did him no good as he was later executed in Somerset.

The main result of the battle was a brief revival in Lancastrian fortunes. Edward IV surrendered to Warwick and was imprisoned but the latter's attempts to run the country soon aroused widespread opposition. Edward was released and regained control while the ambitious Warwick waited for another opportunity.

The Route

1. Start at the crossroads, by the village sign and between the two pubs, and walk along the lane, signposted 'Village Only', to the impressive medieval church. Keep to the left of it along Mill Lane and, where the lane bends right, keep ahead, passing between gateposts and beside a lodge, along a wooded track. The track becomes enclosed and ahead is a fine view over the battlefield. Head gently downhill to cross the River Cherwell, go through a kissing gate and keep ahead across a field. Edgcote's medieval church and the adjacent hall can be seen in front and make a fine composition. Go through another kissing gate, keep ahead to a lane and turn right through the hamlet, passing in front of the hall and church.

2. At a public bridleway sign just beyond a lane on the left, turn left and follow a path in a straight line across a field. The path continues along the left field edge but look out for where you turn left through a waymarked gate, bear right and head in the same direction as before across the next field to emerge onto a tarmac track. Keep ahead towards Edgcote Lodge Farm, heading uphill, and on the brow – just before the track bends right – bear left onto a path. From here there is a superb view over the Cherwell valley and the battle site. The path heads downhill by the left edge of woodland (Old Spinney). At the bottom corner of the wood, go through a gap into the next field and bear right diagonally across it. This is

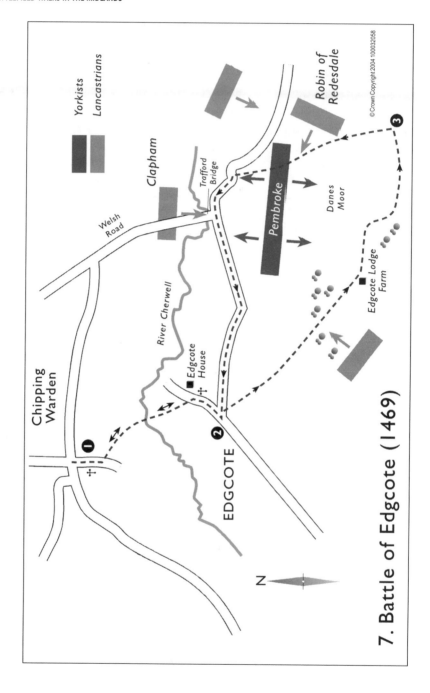

Yorkists
Lancastrians

Robin of Redesdale

Clapham

Trafford Bridge

Welsh Road

Pembroke

Danes Moor

River Cherwell

Edgcote House

Edgcote Lodge Farm

Chipping Warden

EDGCOTE

N

© Crown Copyright 2004 100032058

7. Battle of Edgcote (1469)

the heart of the battlefield where some of the fiercest fighting took place. At a fork, take the left-hand path to continue across the field and on the far side, keep ahead through an area of rough land and long grass, pass through a belt of trees and ford a narrow brook. Keep along the left edge of the next field, heading uphill, going over the brow and descending to a T-junction in the bottom corner.

3. Turn left along the right edge of a field and the track later continues along a left field edge. Where it bends right, keep ahead along the left edge of the field – this part may be overgrown in summer – and go through a fence gap onto a road. Turn left, go round a left bend and the road bends right to cross the River Cherwell at Trafford Bridge. Ahead is the Welsh Road, along which many of Pembroke's Welsh troops escaped after the battle. Do not follow the road to the right over the river but keep ahead along a lane, signposted to Edgcote and Wardington. After 1 mile (1.6km) you reach a T-junction at point 2. Turn right, here rejoining the outward route, and retrace your steps to the start.

8

The Battle of Tewkesbury, 4 May 1471

The Battle of Tewkesbury was fought in the meadows and on the gentle slopes to the south of the town and was easily visible from the tower of its great abbey. The walk goes across the heart of the battle site, partly following a well-signed Battle Trail, and finishes with a relaxing stroll by meadows fringing the rivers Severn and Avon which meet just to the west of the town.

Start: Tewkesbury, by war memorial, grid ref SO893326

Distance: 4 miles (6.4km)

Time: 2 hours

Parking: Tewkesbury

Refreshments: Pubs ands cafes at Tewkesbury

Map: OS Explorer 190 (Malvern Hills & Bredon Hill)

In 1470 Edward IV's fortunes suffered a serious reverse. His former ally, the powerful Warwick the Kingmaker, and his brother, the Duke of Clarence, had joined the Lancastrians. Henry VI was released from the Tower of London and restored to the throne and Edward and his other brother, Richard of Gloucester, were forced to flee to Burgundy. But they returned with an army early in 1471 and, now reconciled with their brother Clarence, inflicted a severe defeat on Warwick and the Lancastrians at Barnet on 14 April. Warwick was killed in that battle, Edward IV was king again and the unfortunate Henry VI returned to the Tower.

On the same day as the battle of Barnet, Henry's wife, Queen Margaret, and her son, Edward Prince of Wales, landed with a small force at Weymouth to rally the Lancastrian cause. Hoping to gain support in Wales, she marched northwards to Bristol and intended

The Norman tower of Tewkesbury's magnificent abbey. The tomb of Edward Prince of Wales, son of Henry VI, who was killed in the battle, lies beneath the tower.

crossing the River Severn into Wales. The nearest bridge was at Gloucester but Edward IV ordered the citizens to close the gates to the Lancastrian army. Pursued by the king, Margaret continued on to Tewkesbury, which occupied a strategic position at the confluence of the Severn and Avon. Here the confrontation took place on the south side of the town.

The Lancastrian forces were probably deployed near Gupshill Manor and the Yorkists were slightly to the south along a low ridge stretching roughly through Stonehouse Farm and Southwick Park to Tewkesbury Park, the latter now a golf course. The Yorkist army was led by the king, Richard of Gloucester and Lord Hastings. The Lancastrian commanders were the Duke of Somerset, Earl of Devon and Lord Wenlock. Somerset, on the right flank of the Lancastrian army, advanced against Richard of Gloucester, on the opposite left flank, but was forced to retreat, caught between Richard's troops and a small force of spearmen sent by Edward to Tewkesbury Park to protect his left flank. Internal bickering now fatally weakened the Lancastrians. Somerset accused Wenlock of not supporting him and, it is alleged, beheaded him in front of his own troops. Driven back by the Yorkists, the Lancastrians fled in panic towards the town, hoping to seek sanctuary in the abbey, but large numbers were killed in Bloody Meadow and while trying to cross the little River Swilgate.

The crushing defeat at Tewkesbury was the final nail in the coffin for the Lancastrian cause. During the retreat, Edward, Prince of Wales, was captured by the Duke of Clarence and killed. Somerset was executed a few days later. Queen Margaret was captured, imprisoned in the Tower of London and later ransomed by the King of France. And after long years of uncertainty and imprisonment, the now pathetic Henry VI was murdered. With the former king and his heir dead and Queen Margaret in prison, Edward IV could at last rule as the undisputed king.

The Route

1. The walk begins by the war memorial in the town centre at the junction of three roads. Walk along Church Street towards the Royal Hop Pole Hotel but, before reaching it, turn left down Lilleys Alley – one of many such alleys in the centre of Tewkesbury – to a road. Turn right towards the abbey, built in the 12th century and a magnificent example of Norman architecture. Although the monastic buildings have disappeared, the great church survived the dissolution of the monasteries in the 16th century as it was bought by the local people for use as their parish church. Beneath the central tower a small plaque indicates the tomb of Henry VI's son, Edward Prince of Wales, killed in the battle.

   Turn left at a T-junction in front of a car park, cross a bridge over the little River Swilgate and, where the lane ends, bear right through gates into a recreation ground, King George's Field. Take the tarmac path gently uphill across it and to the right is a monument to the battle. These fields, then called The Vineyards, occupied part of the battle site and from the monument there is a stunning view of the south side of the abbey. In the top corner of the field, continue along an enclosed tarmac path that emerges onto a road, cross over and, at a fork, take the left-hand track (Conigree Lane).

   Cross a road, keep ahead along an enclosed path and just before the next road, turn right along another enclosed path to a road. Walk along it, keep ahead at a crossroads and, at a T-junction,

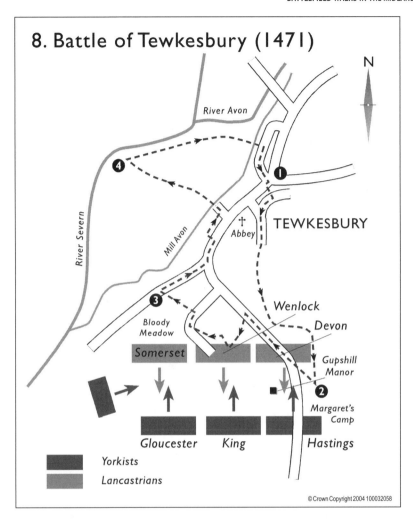

8. Battle of Tewkesbury (1471)

N

River Avon

TEWKESBURY

River Severn

Mill Avon

† Abbey

Wenlock

Devon

Bloody
Meadow

Gupshill
Manor

Somerset

Margaret's
Camp

Gloucester   King   Hastings

Yorkists

Lancastrians

© Crown Copyright 2004 100032058

continue along the enclosed path opposite to a gate. Go through
and walk across rough meadowland to a T-junction in front of a
small tree about 20 yards (18m) ahead.

2. The area around is the site of Margaret's Camp, where the
Lancastrian forces were camped before the battle. At the T-junction, turn right to a gate and footpath post on the edge of the
meadow, go through and turn left along an enclosed tarmac path.
In front is the 15th-century Gupshill Manor, now a pub. Whether

this was where the Lancastrians were deployed or in the no man's land between the rival armies is debateable, but the manor house was certainly in the thick of the fighting.

The path bends first right and then left to emerge onto the busy A38 just to the right of the pub. Turn right and, at public footpath and Battle Trail signs, turn left over a stile and walk along the right edge of a meadow. At the next Battle Trail sign, turn right over a stile, walk along an enclosed tarmac path and, where it bends right, turn left and cross a footbridge. Turn right along the right edge of a meadow, bear left across it to its left edge and in the corner, turn left over a stile onto a lane.

Turn right to a T-junction, turn right again and, at public footpath and Battle Trail signs, turn left through a kissing gate and walk along the right edge of Bloody Meadow. As the name suggests, this was a scene of great carnage as the fleeing Lancastrians were killed in large numbers as they tried to escape from the pursuing and triumphant Yorkist army. There is an information board about the battle here. In the corner of the meadow, follow a path through trees to a T-junction and turn left to a lane.

3. Turn right and, at a T-junction, turn left along the A38 again. At a car park on the edge of the town, turn left along its right edge and bear right, in the direction 'River', along a tarmac path through Victoria Gardens. The path emerges onto a road by Abbey Mill. Turn left beside the mill, at a public footpath sign to Rivers and Severn Ham, cross a footbridge over the Mill Avon and follow a path across the meadowland of Severn Ham to the River Severn.

4. Turn right along its bank and the path curves right to continue beside the River Avon. Cross a footbridge over the Mill Avon again, turn right and the road bends left away from the river and curves right and then left again to return to the start.

What else is there to see?

There is a display about the battle, including a diorama, in the Tewkesbury Museum, housed in a half-timbered medieval building.

9

The Battle of Bosworth, 22 August 1485

Bosworth is possibly the best-preserved battle site in the country. There is an excellent visitor centre, a battle trail with lots of information boards, plenty of car parks and almost the whole of the site is accessible. The route starts by where Richard III's armies were camped, goes over Ambion Hill, from where the whole battlefield can be surveyed, passes through the area that saw the major fighting, visits the alleged site of Richard's death and passes close to where Henry Tudor's troops camped. Most of the walking is across fields and along quiet lanes and there are also short stretches along a canal towpath and through woodland.

Start: Bosworth Battlefield, Cheney Lane car park and picnic site, about half a mile (0.8km) to the west of Sutton Cheney, grid ref SK411005

Distance: 6½ miles (10.5km)

Time: 3½ hours

Parking: Cheney Lane

Refreshments: Café at Whitemoors Antiques and Craft Centre

Map: OS Explorer 232 (Nuneaton & Tamworth)

After the victory at Tewkesbury, it seemed that the Yorkist dynasty was safe but uncertainty and instability returned with the premature death of Edward IV, at the age of forty, in 1483. As the new king, Edward V, was only twelve years old, it was inevitable that there would be some sort of protectorate and the only realistic choice for protector was the king's uncle, Richard, Duke of Gloucester. But Richard wanted the throne for himself. Was it through a personal lust for power – the traditional view – or a genuine belief

King Richard's Well on the battlefield of Bosworth. During the battle, the king is said to have drunk from here.

that at such a time, England needed the sort of strong and firm king-ship that only he could provide? Whatever his motives, Richard arranged for the boy king and his nine-year-old brother, Richard, Duke of York, to be installed in the Tower of London – was it impris-onment or for their safety? – and he was crowned King Richard III.

The dubious circumstances of his accession – and the disappear-ance of the 'Princes in the Tower' – immediately reopened old wounds and the new king was faced with rebellions. Opposition to his rule was based around the likeliest alternative monarch, Henry Tudor, Earl of Richmond, a Welshman and heir to the Lancastrian cause. He was currently in exile in Brittany but with support prom-ised in England and equipped with a force of around 2000 mercenar-ies provided by the King of France, Henry landed in west Wales on 7 August 1485 to claim the English throne.

He marched across Wales and on into the Midlands, gathering support as he went. Richard III based himself at Nottingham Castle and summoned his chief supporters – Duke of Norfolk, Earl of Northumberland and Earl of Surrey – to meet him at Leicester. On 19

August, Richard set out from Nottingham for Leicester and Henry continued his march across the Midlands to Atherstone. The two armies were now close.

Richard arrived in Leicester on 20 August and on the following day carried on to Sutton Cheney where he camped the night before the battle near the base of Ambion Hill. Henry was on the other side of the hill at Whitemoors. Richard had several advantages. By dawn on the day of the battle (22 August), his forces had occupied the top of the hill, they outnumbered the rebel troops and Richard was a vastly more experienced commander than Henry. But the king had serious problems. Some of his supporters, notably Northumberland, were lukewarm and the allegiance of the powerful Stanley family, of crucial significance, was uncertain.

Sir William Stanley secretly supported Henry but Lord Thomas Stanley was in a dilemma as Richard held his son as a hostage to his father's loyalty. With their 4000 men, the Stanleys largely held the key to the outcome of the battle and placed themselves in such a position that they could intervene on either side as the fighting developed.

The southern slopes of Ambion Hill, now mostly covered by woodland, were marshy and Henry's army skirted around the marsh. Norfolk commanded the vanguard of the royal army and led the charge down the slopes of the hill against Henry's vanguard, led by the Earl of Oxford. The fighting was fierce and during the course of it, Norfolk was killed. As the battle continued, Northumberland's rearguard troops made no effort to come to Richard's support and the Stanleys indicated that they were preparing to intervene on the side of Henry. With the rebels now outnumbering the royal troops, Richard bravely led a charge, possibly to prevent the Stanleys linking up with Henry. During the charge, the king was unhorsed and struck down and died fighting gallantly. After the king's death, the royal armies lost the will to fight and either surrendered or fled. Northumberland's troops, who had played virtually no part in the fighting, left the scene. According to tradition, Richard III's crown was found on the branches of a thorn bush and placed on Henry's head, appropriately by Lord Stanley.

Bosworth ranks as one of the most decisive battles in English history. It was the final battle of the thirty-year Wars of the Roses. Richard III was the last of the Plantagenets and the last English king

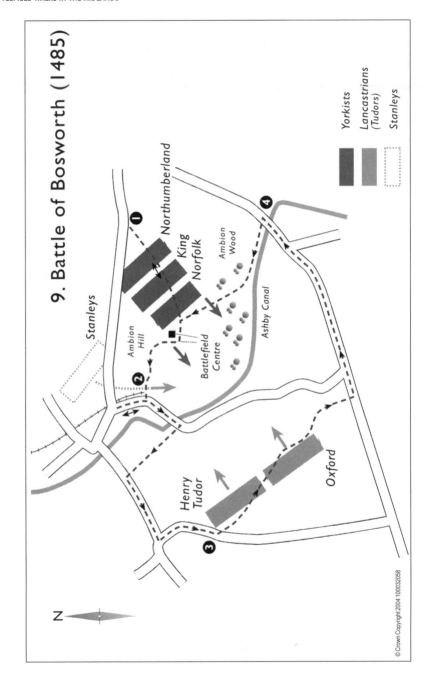

9. Battle of Bosworth (1485)

Stanleys

Northumberland

King Norfolk

Ambion Hill

Battlefield Centre

Ambion Wood

Ashby Canal

Henry Tudor

Oxford

Yorkists

Lancastrians (Tudors)

Stanleys

N

© Crown Copyright 2004 100032058

to be killed leading his troops into battle. Henry, founder of the powerful Tudor dynasty, was crowned King Henry VII and his victory at Bosworth was to pave the way for such momentous events as the Reformation, the Elizabethan age and the ultimate union of the English and Scottish crowns.

The Route

1. Go through the gate at the far end of the car park and walk up the gentle slopes of Ambion Hill, along the right edge of a succession of fields and through a series of gates, to the Bosworth Battlefield Visitor Centre. As Richard III's army was camped at Sutton Cheney the night before the battle, it is likely that you are following in the footsteps of some of his troops.

   Continue past the Visitor Centre, following the direction of a fingerpost to Shenton Station and, at a T-junction by the next fingerpost, turn left for a short detour to King Richard's Well. You reach the well by turning right at the next T-junction. Now topped by a stone pyramid, the king is supposed to have drunk from the spring here during the battle. Return to the last fingerpost, by Battle Trail Information Board 2, and keep ahead, still following signs to Shenton Station. The path bends right, then bends left through a gate and heads downhill, curving left and keeping along the bottom edge of the field. Continue along an enclosed path, go through a gate, cross a path and go through another gate to Shenton station. This area was in the thick of the battle and the scene of some of the fiercest fighting.

2. Cross the railway line and walk through the car park to a lane. Turn right here for another brief detour to King Richard's Field, taking the enclosed path that runs parallel to the road at a Battlefield symbol. It was here, by the stream just in front of the memorial stone, that Richard is alleged to have been killed.

   Return to Shenton station and continue along the lane. Just after crossing a bridge over the Ashby Canal, turn right through a gate, at a public footpath sign, and walk across a field. On the far side, cross a footbridge over a brook, keep ahead across the next field, between an avenue of trees, and go through a gate onto a lane. Turn left through the hamlet of Shenton, passing the hall on the left and the church on the right, to a T-junction and turn left, in the White Moors direction. Walk along the winding lane, passing the Whitemoors Antiques and Craft Centre. Henry's army was camped around here the night before the battle.

3. At a public footpath sign, turn left over a stile. Walk along the left edge of two fields and after climbing a stile, continue straight across the next field, making for a waymarked stile on the far side. Climb it, veer slightly right across a field, climb a stile, walk along the left edge of the next field and climb another stile to the left of farm buildings. Continue along an enclosed path, climb a stile, bear right across a field and on the far side, climb two more stiles in quick succession. Continue straight across the next field and climb a stile onto a road. Turn left for 1 mile (1.6km) to Sutton Wharf Bridge.

4. Just beyond the bridge, turn left over a stile into a car park. Walk along a track, signposted to Battlefield Visitor Centre and, where the track bends left, keep ahead across grass, turning first left and then right to go through a kissing gate. Continue along a path beside the Ashby Canal and, after the next kissing gate, you enter Ambion Wood. The wood did not exist at the time of the battle and this was open, marshy ground. Follow a clear and winding path gently uphill through the trees and go through a kissing gate to leave the wood. Continue across a field to go through another kissing gate and keep ahead to the Visitor Centre. Turn right at a fingerpost, in the Sutton Cheney direction, here picking up the outward route, and retrace your steps to the start.

What else is there to see?

There is a memorial to Richard III in Sutton Cheney church, where he is alleged to have worshipped on his way to the battle.

10

Richard III at Leicester, August 1485

The walk links most of the places in Leicester associated with Richard III in 1485, as well as including other places of interest in the city. The short route is a circuit of the city centre; the full walk includes an optional 'there and back' detour, mainly alongside the River Soar and Grand Union Canal, to the attractive Abbey Park which contains the site of the abbey in which Cardinal Wolsey died.

Start: Leicester, Town Hall Square, grid ref SK587044

Distance: 4 miles (6.4km); Shorter walk 1½ miles (2.4km)

Time: 2 hours (1 hour for short walk)

Parking: Plenty of car parks in Leicester city centre but best to use the Park and Ride scheme

Refreshments: Pubs, restaurants and cafes in Leicester, café in Abbey Park

Map: OS Explorer 233 (Leicester & Hinckley) or town map of Leicester

Leicester played a major role in the final days of the Wars of the Roses during the summer of 1485, both before and after the crucial battle of Bosworth. Richard III had visited the town on several occasions while Duke of Gloucester as the castle was a convenient place to stay while journeying between the north and south of England.

On 20 August 1485, he arrived in Leicester on his way to deal with the threat to his throne posed by Henry Tudor, whose rebel army was nearby. He did not stay at the castle on this occasion but at the Blue Boar Inn, the site of which is on Highcross Street. On the morning of 21 August, he left the town via Bow Bridge on his way to do battle with Henry and, according to legend, his spur hit a stone as he was crossing the bridge. An old woman in the crowd saw this as a bad omen and allegedly predicted that the king's head would strike the same stone on the way back. On the following day, after defeat and death at Bosworth, his body was brought back across the bridge for eventual burial in the chapel of Greyfriars monastery.

Some years later, in the violence that took place during the dissolution of the monasteries, it is believed that his bones were dug up and thrown over Bow Bridge into the River Soar. Richard III is therefore one of the few Kings of England for whom there is no known grave but nowadays there are plenty of reminders of him throughout the city of Leicester.

The Route

1. From Town Hall Square, walk along Horsefair Street, continue along Millstone Lane and, where the road bends right, keep ahead under a subway, following signs to De Montfort University and Castle Park. Walk along The Newarke, keeping to the left of Newarke Houses Museum. At Castle View, turn right, passing under the southern gateway of Castle Yard, for a brief detour to see St Mary le Castro Church and the façade of the Great Hall of Leicester Castle. The church was originally the castle chapel and Geoffrey Chaucer married his second wife here. Although much altered and rebuilt over the years, the Great Hall, originally built in the 12th century, is the only surviving part of the medieval castle.

   Return to The Newarke, turn right and turn right again through gates to enter Castle Gardens. Walk through the gardens – the River Soar is on the left and the 11th-century motte (mound) of the castle is to the right – and just before emerging onto a road, you pass a statue to Richard III. Cross the dual carriageway, turn left along St Augustine Road and cross the first bridge over the River Soar.

2. Keep ahead and cross Richard III Road to the next bridge, which is Bow Bridge. Richard rode across this bridge en route for Bosworth, his body returned to Leicester over the same bridge and it was from here that his bones were later thrown into the

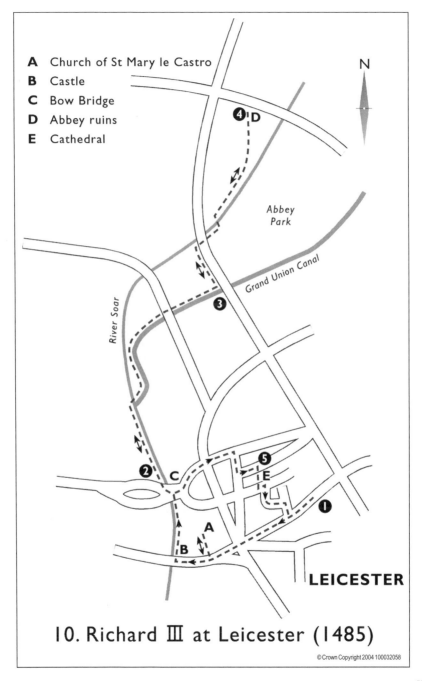

A Church of St Mary le Castro
B Castle
C Bow Bridge
D Abbey ruins
E Cathedral

N

Abbey Park

Grand Union Canal

River Soar

LEICESTER

10. Richard Ⅲ at Leicester (1485)

© Crown Copyright 2004 100032058

river. Retrace your steps to the first bridge and keep ahead for the shorter walk. For the full walk – to Abbey Park and the abbey ruins – turn left before crossing the bridge and take the riverside path.

Turn right across the first footbridge – above a weir – pass under a bridge and bear right to cross another footbridge over another weir. Cross a bridge and continue along the towpath of the Grand Union Canal to North Lock. Pass under a road bridge (Northgate Street), keep along the

The statue of Richard III in Leicester's Castle Park is near to Bow Bridge from where, it is said, the king's remains were later thrown into the River Soar.

towpath and, at the next road bridge (St Margaret's Way), turn left up steps to the road.

3. Continue along a footpath and cycleway parallel to the road, curving right to pass under a road bridge to join the River Soar again. At a sign to Abbey Park and Birstall, turn left to cross a bridge over the river and turn right to continue along the other bank. Pass under an arch in a brick wall and keep by the river through Abbey Park to the next bridge. Turn left towards the statue of Cardinal Wolsey in front of the Abbey Tea Rooms and immediately turn right under an arch and walk across the grass to the site of Leicester Abbey. It was built in the 12th century and fell into ruin after the dissolution of the monasteries in the 1530s.

Cardinal Wolsey died at the abbey in 1528 while on his way to London and his body was buried here.

4. Retrace your steps along the river and canal to St Augustine Road and turn left to rejoin the shorter walk at point 2. Walk towards the Holiday Inn and follow St Nicholas Circle to the left, passing to the right of the Jewry Wall Roman site and St Nicholas Church. The Jewry Wall, part of a public baths complex, is one of the highest surviving Roman walls in Britain. There is a museum with mosaics on the site. At a 'Trail' sign, bear right to cross the road, heading towards the spire of Leicester Cathedral. Keep ahead over another road, walk along the side of St Nicholas Place, turn right, following signs to Guildhall and Cathedral, towards the medieval Wyggestons House and turn left into Guildhall Lane.

5. Turn right along St Martins West, passing between the Guildhall and cathedral. The picturesque, half-timbered, 14th-century Guildhall was Leicester's town hall until 1876. Leicester Cathedral is a restored mainly 15th-century building. It was originally a parish church and was raised to cathedral status in 1927. Inside is a memorial to Richard III. Turn left into Peacock Lane and turn right into New Street. If you look in the car park on the right – just behind the attendant's hut – you can see a small piece of stone. This is believed to be the only remaining part of Greyfriars monastery, in which the body of Richard III was originally buried. At a T-junction, turn left into Friar Lane, turn right along Berridge Street and a left turn into Millstone Lane returns you to the start.

11

The Battle of Stoke Field, 16 June 1487

The only access to the site is by walking along the track known as Humber Lane, which ascends the ridge on which the rebel armies were positioned. There are no public footpaths across the battlefield and a circular walk is impossible. Therefore the route uses the lane from the village to East Stoke church and then goes along a track to the banks of the River Trent before retracing steps to the start.

Start: East Stoke, crossroads in village centre, grid ref SK754496

Distance: 3 miles (4.8km)

Time: 1½ hours

Parking: Roadside parking in School Lane at East Stoke

Refreshments: Pub at East Stoke

Map: OS Explorer 271 (Newark-on-Trent)

Although Bosworth is generally regarded as the final battle of the Wars of the Roses, Henry VII still faced opposition from former Yorkist supporters and from pretenders who claimed to be one of the Princes in the Tower or other members of the former royal family. One such pretender was Lambert Simnel, who claimed to be Edward, Earl of Warwick, the son of the Duke of Clarence who had been brother to both Edward IV and Richard III. He was sent to Ireland, where he was crowned 'Edward VI' in Dublin, and with the support of Irish troops, German and Swiss mercenaries and rebel Yorkists who had come to Ireland from Flanders, he sailed across the Irish Sea and landed on the west coast of England, near Barrow-in-Furness.

The rebels marched into Lancashire and across the Pennines into

Yorkshire. From there, they turned southwards into Nottinghamshire and reached Southwell. Henry VII meanwhile had marched north into the Midlands to Nottingham and continued on towards Newark. Only a few miles and the broad waters of the River Trent separated the two armies. It is thought that the rebels, led by the Earl of Lincoln, probably forded the Trent at Fiskerton and then occupied a ridge to the west of the village of East Stoke about 3 miles (4.8km) south of Newark. The king's army was drawn up across the Fosse Way – now the A46 – which runs through the village.

The church at East Stoke. A stone at the base of the tower commemorates those who were killed in the Battle of Stoke Field.

There are few details of the battle. Lincoln launched an attack on the royal vanguard, led by the Earl of Oxford, and threw the royal army into confusion. Oxford was saved only by the arrival of reinforcements. As the royal troops counter-attacked, the rebels were pushed back. Although the German and Swiss mercenaries fought well and stood their ground, the undisciplined Irish troops fled in confusion. Henry's forces pursued the fleeing rebels and there was much slaughter as they fled over the ridge – now thickly-wooded – through a gully known as Red Gutter. Many drowned trying to escape by swimming across the river. Lord Lovell, one of the leading conspirators against the king, is one who is alleged to have successfully swum across the Trent only to die later of starvation, while hiding in a secret chamber in his manor house at Minster Lovell in Oxfordshire. Lincoln was killed during the battle and Lambert Simnel was captured but was spared execution. Instead he was employed as a cook in the royal kitchens.

Despite his victory, Henry VII's position was not finally secure and it was several years before the spectre of renewed civil war was ended.

The Route

1. Start by walking along School Lane and continue along Church Lane, passing under a brick bridge to East Stoke church. The church, which stands on a ridge next to Stoke Hall, dates mainly from the late 17th and early 18th centuries apart from the medieval west tower. Near the base of the tower there is a stone commemorating those who were killed in the battle. The lane curves left below a wooded ridge and, where it bends right, keep ahead along a track, at a public bridleway sign. It was over this ridge on the left, especially through the gully of Red Gutter, that many of the rebel forces tried to escape after the battle and in 1825 the owner of Stoke Hall found large numbers of skeletons both here and in the vicinity of the church.

   The grassy track bears slightly right to continue in a straight line across fields – it is slightly raised above the field on the right – to the River Trent. Keep ahead by the river, go through an old hedgebank and continue to the corner of the next field. After the battle, some of the defeated rebels may well have tried to swim across the river near here in order to escape from their pursuers.

2. From here, retrace your steps to the village but before returning to the crossroads, turn right along School Lane – later Humber Lane – for a detour of just over half a mile (0.8km). The lane soon becomes an enclosed track, which leads almost to the top of the ridge that was occupied by the rebel forces and gives the best views over the site of the battle. Return to the village and turn right at a T-junction to return to the start.

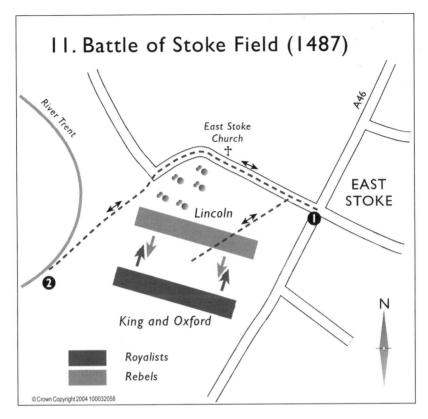

11. Battle of Stoke Field (1487)

River Trent

A46

East Stoke
Church

EAST
STOKE

Lincoln

King and Oxford

N

Royalists
Rebels

© Crown Copyright 2004 100032058

What else is there to see?

Walk or drive along the lane from East Stoke to where it ends at the river opposite the village of Fiskerton. This is the likeliest place where the rebel army forded the Trent on their way to the battle and also where some tried to escape back across the river after their defeat.

12

Charles I at Nottingham, August 1642

The main theme on this walk is the official start of the Civil War between Charles I and Parliament, an event which took place outside the walls of Nottingham Castle in August 1642. The route also takes in other sites that have a connection with that conflict and major places of interest in the city centre.

Start: Nottingham, Old Market Square, grid ref SK573399

Distance: 1½ miles (2.4km)

Time: 1 hour

Parking: Plenty of car parks in Nottingham city centre but best to use the Park and Ride scheme

Refreshments: Pubs and cafes at Nottingham

Map: OS Explorer 260 (Nottingham) or town map of Nottingham

As relations between King and Parliament deteriorated in the spring of 1642, Charles I left London because the capital was so hostile to him and journeyed northwards. Initially he based himself in York. Throughout the spring and summer both sides were gathering armies and preparing for war.

In August, Charles moved southwards, possibly en route for London, first to Leicester and on to Coventry but then retreated to Nottingham. The town had a powerful royal castle and controlled an important crossing point on the River Trent. He also needed to acquire more troops before thinking of marching on London and before reaching the town, he issued a proclamation on 12 August urging all able bodied men within a 20-mile radius to come forward and join his cause. He arrived in Nottingham on 19 August but as the castle was currently in a somewhat dilapidated state, Charles stayed at the now-vanished Thurland Hall, the town house of the Earl of Clare, one of his supporters.

Although it was basically a formality, the king's raising of the standard outside the castle walls at around 6pm on the evening of 22 August marked the official commencement of hostilities. That night it blew down in a storm – seen by some as an unlucky omen – and the ceremony was repeated on the two successive evenings. Despite his appeal for support, Charles managed to recruit only about 300 men from a reluctant and mainly pro-Parliament local area. Disappointed by the lukewarm response and with strong Parliamentary forces quite close, the king left Nottingham on 13 September and moved on to what he hoped was more promising and loyal territory around Shrewsbury.

The gatehouse of Nottingham Castle. During the Civil War, this Parliamentary stronghold was attacked five times by Royalist troops.

Throughout the Civil War Nottingham Castle was held for Parliament by Colonel John Hutchinson and was attacked five times by Royalist troops. The most serious of these was in September 1643 when Royalists from Newark, led by a cousin of Hutchinson, occupied the town for five days and bombarded the castle from the tower of the nearby St Nicholas' Church. After the Royalists retreated, Hutchinson demolished the church in order to prevent a repetition. He also ordered the demolition of the castle at the end of the war.

The Route

1. The walk begins in the Old Market Square in front of the Council House. With your back to the Council House, walk across the square and continue along St James's Street. Cross Maid Marian Way, keep ahead and turn left into St James's Terrace. On a wall opposite is a plaque recording that it was near here that Charles I raised his standard on 22 August 1642 to signal the start of the Civil War. Continue down to the gatehouse of Nottingham Castle.

2. There is another plaque in the castle grounds commemorating the raising of the royal standard. Apart from the heavily restored gatehouse, the Parliamentarians razed the medieval castle to the ground after the Civil War and the Duke of Newcastle built a fine 17th-century mansion on the site. This in turn was burnt down in the Reform Bill riots of 1831 and reconstructed later in the 19th century as a museum and art gallery. Keep ahead down Castle Road, passing a statue of Robin Hood beneath the castle walls, and by the Lace Centre turn left into Castle Gate. If you continue a short way down Castle Road you come to the picturesque Trip to Jerusalem, which claims to date from 1189 and to be the oldest inn in England. Some of the rooms are caves hewn out of the sandstone of the castle rock. Return to Castle Gate, walk along it and recross Maid Marian Way.

3. On the corner is St Nicholas' Church, whose tower was used by the Royalists in 1643 to bombard the castle. This resulted in its demolition but it was subsequently rebuilt in brick between 1671 and 1682. In the churchyard is the gravestone of Lawrence Collin, a Parliamentary master gunner in the castle during the Civil War, who died at the ripe old age of 91 in 1704. A few yards to the left is another of Nottingham's medieval inns, the Salutation which dates from 1204. In 1642 it was used by Charles I as his recruiting centre. Keep ahead along Castle Gate and then Low Pavement to Weekday Cross, where you enter the Lace Market area. In the 19th century this became the centre of Nottingham's flourishing lace industry and many of the huge and imposing Victorian warehouses remain. Continue along Middle Pavement and High Pavement to the 18th-century Shire Hall and St Mary's Church.

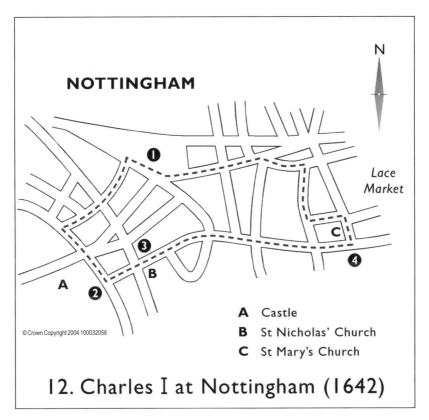

NOTTINGHAM

Lace Market

© Crown Copyright 2004 100032058

A Castle
B St Nicholas' Church
C St Mary's Church

12. Charles I at Nottingham (1642)

4. St Mary's, the mother church of Nottingham, is a fine example of a prosperous 15th-century town church. By the church, turn left into Stoney Street and left again into Broadway, passing some of the most impressive of the Lace Market buildings. At a T-junction turn right along St Mary's Gate and turn left at the next T-junction. Turn right and immediately left to continue along Victoria Street back to the Old Market Square.

What else is there to see?

There is a display about the Civil War in Nottingham in the Castle Museum

13

The Battle of Edgehill, 23 October 1642

The actual battlefield is – perhaps appropriately – on land currently owned by the Ministry of Defence and is therefore inaccessible. However most of the site can be seen from the wooded ridge of Edge Hill that you climb up to on the first stage of the walk. The route includes outstanding views over a large slice of south Warwickshire, pleasant woodland and two attractive, stone-built villages.

Start: Radway, village centre, grid ref SP372484

Distance: 4 miles (6.4km)

Time: 2 hours

Parking: Roadside parking at Radway

Refreshments: Pub at Ratley, pub at Edgehill

Map: OS Explorer 206 (Edge Hill & Fenny Compton)

Edgehill was the first battle of the Civil War and took place two months after Charles I had signalled the start of the war by unfurling his standard outside the walls of Nottingham Castle. Charles had spent the time in the Midlands gathering together an army ready for an assault on London, the key to a quick victory, and he began his march on the capital on 12 October. The Parliamentary army under the Earl of Essex moved to the Midlands to keep an eye on the king and based itself at Worcester.

Charles gave Essex the slip and marched towards Warwick. Essex set off in pursuit and the two armies met near Edge Hill, a 3 mile (4.8km) long ridge which rises abruptly to around 700 feet (213m) above the south Warwickshire plain and commands a main route from Warwick to London. Here the king decided to give battle, as it was too risky to continue southwards with a Parliamentary army in his rear.

Edge Hill Tower, now the Castle Inn, overlooks the site of the battle

Charles himself and his nephew, Prince Rupert, a brilliant young cavalry officer, led the Royalist army. Both armies had around 15,000 men but the Royalists were more experienced. On the night before the battle Charles and his army occupied the ridge and their descent from the hill on the following morning marked the start of hostilities. Charles' position was nearest the foot of the hill, just to the north of the village of Radway. Essex and the Parliamentary army were drawn up a little further north, nearer to Kineton.

The battle began with a charge by Rupert's cavalry, which was successful. He chased his opponents off the field and pursued them to Kineton and beyond. Wilmot, who led the other flank of the Royalist cavalry, also led a successful charge. Fierce and prolonged close fighting followed between the rival infantry forces during which no quarter was given and losses were high. As the battle progressed, confusion and tiredness crept in and the late return of Rupert's cavalry to the battlefield made no difference as neither his men nor horses were in any condition to fight. With the coming of darkness the battle petered out and both armies withdrew.

At this early stage in the conflict, neither side was willing to risk an all out battle and the general consensus is that the result was indecisive. Essex pulled back to Warwick and Charles, having spent

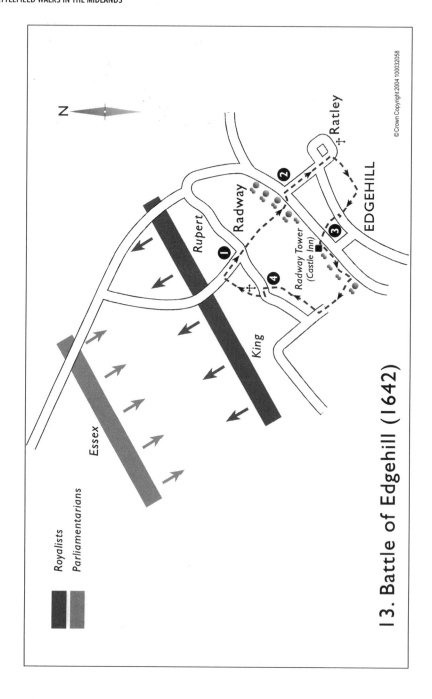

© Crown Copyright 2004 100032058

13. Battle of Edgehill (1642)

the night on the battlefield at Kings Leys Barn – about half a mile (0.8km) north of Radway – moved to Oxford, which became his headquarters for the remainder of the war.

The Route

1. Start at the T-junction in the centre of Radway and facing the bus shelter, turn left. At a public footpath sign, turn right along a track that narrows to a path and continues to a kissing gate. Go through, walk along an enclosed path, go through another kissing gate and keep ahead towards the trees that crown the ridge of Edge Hill. Before reaching a kissing gate, look behind and the whole battlefield is stretched out before you. Go through the kissing gate to enter the woodland, turn left at a T-junction and, at a fork immediately ahead, take the right-hand upper path. Ascend a flight of steps – known as Jacobs Ladder – continue uphill, climb more steps and the path emerges onto a road at the top of the ridge.

2. Turn left and almost immediately turn right along a lane sign-posted to Ratley. Descend into the small village and keep ahead down High Street to where the lane bends left. Follow it around the bend to visit the medieval church and old pub but the route continues to the right along a track. In front of the gates to Manor Farm, turn right to climb a stone stile and bear right uphill, by a wall on the right.

   At the wall corner, keep ahead downhill to a stile, climb it and continue uphill across the next field to a stile at its far narrow end. To the right is a fine view of the earthworks of a motte and bailey castle. After climbing the stile, turn right along the right edge of a field and keep ahead along an enclosed track to a lane. Turn right, turn left at a public footpath sign and walk along an enclosed path, which later bends right and then left to emerge onto the ridge top road again in the village of Edgehill.

3. Turn left towards the Castle Inn but almost immediately turn right down steps, at a public footpath sign, and continue along a path which passes to the right of the inn. Sanderson Miller of Radway Grange built the battlemented Castle Inn, originally known as Edge Hill or Radway Tower, in 1746-50. It stands on the site where Charles I raised his standard before the start of the

battle. At a waymarked post, keep ahead downhill through the trees and the path bends left and continues down to a crossways. Turn left along a pleasant, winding and undulating path – there are steps in places – to a T-junction and turn sharp right downhill along a sunken path. This is an old routeway called King John's Lane.

On emerging onto the end of a lane, keep ahead and, at a public footpath post, turn right through a gate by a house and walk along the left edge of a field to a kissing gate. Go through, keep ahead across the next field and the path bears left to a stile in the corner. Climb it, keep ahead and go through a kissing gate. Continue along an enclosed path, passing between houses and cottages, to a lane and turn left to a T-junction.

4. Turn left again, passing Radway church, built in 1866 on the site of its medieval predecessor. Inside is an effigy to Captain Henry Kingsmill who was killed in the battle of Edgehill. Where the lane bends left, turn right, at a public footpath sign, and walk along a track to a stile. Climb it and walk along the right edge of a field. This is about the nearest point on the route to the battle site, which is over to the left.

Go through a gate, keep ahead across a field, go through another gate, continue across the next field but look out for where you have to turn right over a stile. Continue parallel to the left edge of the next field to a stile, climb it and keep ahead to climb another one. Continue to the next one and after climbing that, walk through a belt of trees to a lane and turn right to return to the start.

What else is there to see?

There is a monument to the battle at the side of the B4086 about 1 ¼ miles (2 km) to the east of Kineton roughly in line with where the Parliamentary forces were deployed.

14

The Battle of Cropredy Bridge, 29 June 1644

Apart from the construction of the Oxford Canal and the fact that the River Cherwell must be both narrower and shallower, the battlefield landscape has changed little since the 17th century and is still mostly covered by fields. The walk encircles the site, which lies between the villages of Cropredy, Wardington and Williamscot, and includes the three main focal points of the conflict, all of which controlled crossing points over the river – Cropredy Bridge, Hays Bridge and the ford at the now vanished Slat Mill.

Start: Cropredy, Sports Ground car park, grid ref SP472465

Distance: 7 miles (11.3km) Shorter walk 5½ miles (8.9km)

Time: 3½ hours (2½ hours for shorter walk)

Parking: Cropredy

Refreshments: Pubs and café at Cropredy, pub at Wardington

Map: OS Explorer 206 (Edge Hill & Fenny Compton)

The battle was quite a complex affair, raging to and fro throughout the day, with attacks and counter-attacks and several twists and turns. It could have gone either way but the eventual result was a Royalist victory.

In 1644, the advance of Parliamentary armies in Oxfordshire made the king's headquarters at Oxford vulnerable and Charles I despatched troops to deal with the danger. He moved to Banbury and then turned northwards towards Daventry, marching along the eastern side of the River Cherwell. At the same time, a Parliamentary force under Waller more or less kept pace with him along the west-

A fine panoramic view over the site of the Battle of Cropredy Bridge, from the south

ern side of the river. Waller camped at Great Bourton near Cropredy and, as only the river separated the rival armies, the three crossing points in the vicinity over the Cherwell – the bridge at Cropredy, Hays Bridge and the ford at Slat Mill – were of vital importance, especially as Parliamentary reinforcements were nearby.

Charles therefore sent a small advance force to secure the bridge at Cropredy. He also marched north to Hays Bridge to try and inter-cept the Parliamentary reinforcements and prevent them from link-ing up with Waller. This opened up a gap in the Royalist forces, which Waller was quick to exploit. He launched a two-pronged attack. One Parliamentary force forded the Cherwell at Slat Mill and another stormed across Cropredy Bridge. The Royalists were pushed back and retreated towards Hays Bridge but now it was the turn of the divided Parliamentary forces to be caught between two Royalist armies. A determined Royalist counter-offensive halted Waller's advance and pushed his armies back over the river. There was particularly heavy and fierce fighting around Cropredy Bridge.

To add to Waller's problems, the king marched to Williamscot and from there his artillery bombarded the Parliamentary position on Bourton Hill. Although the Royalists failed to capture the bridge at Cropredy and Waller escaped, it was a decisive victory for Charles. Parliamentary losses were much greater and the Royalist stronghold at Oxford was safe.

The Route

1. Turn left out of the car park and cross Cropredy Bridge over the River Cherwell. There is a stone commemorating the battle on the south parapet and much of the fiercest fighting took place in its vicinity. Keep ahead to the canal bridge and a brief detour over it brings you into the attractive village of Cropredy, which has thatched cottages, two pubs and a medieval church. In the south aisle of the church, there is some replica armour of the battle – the original pieces, found after the battle, were stolen and never recovered.

   The main route continues down steps in front of the canal bridge to the towpath of the Oxford Canal. Turn right and after passing under the first bridge (152), turn sharp right up to a lane and turn left. To the right is a fine view across the river of the battle site. The lane follows the river around a right curve.

2. When you are beside a wall on the left, look out for where you turn right through a gate and cross a bridge over the Cherwell. Immediately turn left through another gate and walk along the left edge of a field. The path later veers slightly right to a waymarked gate. Go through this, cross a footbridge, keep ahead across the next field and on the far side, turn left over another footbridge.

   Bear right to continue across a succession of fields, heading gently uphill and curving right to continue along a left field edge to the corner. Go through a hedge gap, walk along the left edge of the next field, go through a gate and continue along an enclosed path, passing to the left of a vehicle workshop building. Keep ahead along a tarmac drive, climb a stile and the drive emerges onto the A361 in the village of Wardington.

3. If doing the full walk, turn left along the road to Hays Bridge, a distance of about three-quarters of a mile (1.2km). This was where the Royalists halted the Parliamentary advance and

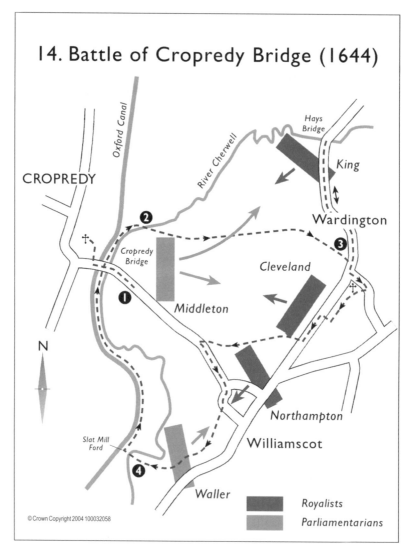

14. Battle of Cropredy Bridge (1644)

Oxford Canal

River Cherwell

Hays Bridge

King

CROPREDY

Wardington

❷

Cropredy Bridge

Cleveland

❸

❶

Middleton

N

Northampton

Slat Mill Ford

Williamscot

❹

Waller

Royalists

Parliamentarians

© Crown Copyright 2004 100032058

launched their successful counter-attack. From the bridge, retrace your steps to Wardington and pick up the shorter walk. For the short walk, turn right along the main road and take the first lane on the left to the church. At a public footpath sign where the lane bends right, turn right through a gate and walk through the churchyard, passing to the left of the fine medieval church.

Go through a gate on the far side and keep ahead, initially by the churchyard wall and later by a hedge on the left, to a waymarked post. Keep ahead across the field – there is rough grass and no visible path at this point – and look out for a half-hidden stile on the far side. Climb it, turn right along the right field edge and climb a stile onto the A361 again. Turn left and, at a public footpath sign to Cropredy, turn right through a hedge gap and head gently downhill across a field. The isolated ash tree which is passed is the successor of a tree by which, it is alleged, Charles I dined on the day of the battle.

Go through a gate in the corner, keep along the left edge of the next field and look out for where you veer slightly left to go through a gate onto a road. Turn sharp left into Williamscot and take the first lane on the right, signposted as a No Through Road. The king is reputed to have slept in a cottage here after the battle. Where the lane bends left, bear right beside a waymarked gate and walk along a track to a stile. Climb it, continue along the track, go through a gate and walk along the left edge of a field. Turn right in front of a gate, continue downhill along the left field edge, go through a gate and keep ahead across the next field, making for a waymarked gate on the far side. After going through it, continue across a field and cross a footbridge over the River Cherwell.

4. This is the site of Slat Mill. In 1644 there was no footbridge but the Cherwell could be forded here. It was one of the vital strategic crossing points on the river and witnessed heavy fighting. Keep ahead across the next field to a canal bridge, climb a stile beside it, descend steps to the towpath and turn right to pass under the bridge. Follow the canal back to Cropredy and, in front of bridge 153, bear right up to a road. Turn right, crossing Cropredy Bridge again, to return to the start.

15

The Battle of Naseby, 14 June 1645

Although there are no public footpaths across the site, almost the whole of the battlefield of Naseby – little changed since the time of the Civil War – can be surveyed from the monument to the north of Naseby village. The route does a short circuit of the village, visiting a battle museum and obelisk, before heading along a lane to the monument where there is an information board.

Start: Naseby, by the church, grid ref SP688783

Distance: 4½ miles (7.2km)

Time: 2 hours

Parking: Roadside parking at Naseby

Refreshments: Pubs at Naseby

Map: OS Explorer 223 (Northampton & Market Harborough)

During the winter of 1644-45, the Parliamentary army was reorganised, modernised and made more efficient. It comprised around 22,000 well-paid, well-disciplined and professional men and became known as the New Model Army. Sir Thomas Fairfax was its Commander-in-Chief and Oliver Cromwell became its cavalry leader. The Battle of Naseby was its first major test.

In the spring of 1645, both the Royalists under Rupert and Parliament's New Model Army, led by Fairfax, were following each other around the Midlands keeping a wary eye on each other. One of the actions of the Royalist army was to sack Leicester and the New Model Army marched to regain it. The two armies met near the village of Naseby and Charles chose to give battle on the high ground to the north of the village and just to the south of Market Harborough. The Royalists occupied the low ridge of Dust Hill. The

New Model Army was just to the south – along the ridge of Red Hill or Fenny Hill – and advanced northwards from Naseby. The scene of the battle was the low ground in between, Broadmoor, and the battlefront stretched for about 1 mile (1.6km) on a west-east axis.

The Parliamentarians had a great numerical advantage, numbering around 14,000 men compared with Royalist forces of around 9,000. Rupert's initial cavalry charge was a success, routing Ireton's troops and pursuing them off the field, but he had only defeated part of Ireton's force and his absence from the field gravely weakened the Royalist infantry. Cromwell's successful counter-charge cancelled out the temporary advantage of Rupert's charge and as the battle continued, the superior numbers of the Parliamentarians began to tell. Cromwell's charge and the presence of Ireton's remaining cavalry troops caused the Royalist cavalry to flee from the battle and the deserted and outnumbered infantry, despite fighting with great courage and tenacity, were forced ultimately to surrender after heavy losses. Rupert's delayed return was too late to be of any real help.

It was the New Model Army's first major battle and resulted in one of the most decisive victories of the war. Parliamentary casualties were far less than those of their opponents but Charles had lost most of his infantry soldiers – about 4,000 were killed – and had few armed forces left. He now had virtually no chance of winning the war.

The Route

1. Start at the village green by the church and Fitzgèrald Arms and walk along Church Street, passing to the right of the fine medieval church. Turn left along a lane called Nutcote (signposted to Battle and Farm Museum) and keep ahead all the time, ignoring side turns, to the museum entrance. Almost opposite the entrance, turn left into Catton Close and, where the road ends, go through a kissing gate and walk across a field – there is no visible path – to another kissing gate on the far side. After going through it, bear slightly right along an overgrown but discernible path through woodland and scrub to a public footpath sign and continue along the left edge of a field. Go through a hedge gap, keep along the left edge of the next field and bear left to a kissing

Looking north over the site of the Battle of Naseby, to where the Royalist army was deployed. This was the scene of Charles I's heaviest defeat.

gate in the corner. Go through, turn left back into the village and take the first lane on the right, signposted to Battle Obelisk. The obelisk, which was erected in 1823, is about ¼ mile (0.4km) along this lane.

2. Retrace your steps to the road junction and turn right to return to the start by Naseby church (point 1). This completes the short circuit of the village. To get to the actual site of the battle, bear right along a lane and take the first lane on the right, signposted to Sibbertoft and Monument. The lane crosses the A14 and heads gently uphill to a small lay-by. Turn left through a kissing gate and a path leads to the monument and information board.

3. The monument was put up in 1936 but the information board wrongly indicates that it is roughly in line with the Parliamentary position where Cromwell launched his charge. It is generally believed now that the Parliamentary army was a little way to the south on Red Hill and therefore the monument lies in the heart of the battle site between the two armies. From here, retrace your steps down the lane to the start.

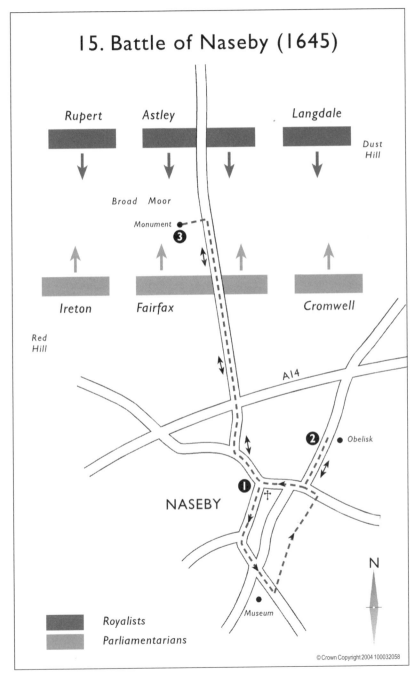

15. Battle of Naseby (1645)

Rupert

Astley

Langdale

Dust Hill

Broad Moor

Monument

❸

Ireton

Fairfax

Cromwell

Red Hill

A14

❷ ● Obelisk

❶

NASEBY

N

Museum

Royalists

Parliamentarians

© Crown Copyright 2004 100032058

16

The Battle of Stow, 21 March 1646

From the centre of Stow-on-the-Wold, scene of much fighting and bloodshed at the end of the battle, the route goes through the attractive village of Broadwell to Donnington, near the main battle site. The return leg follows what is likely to be the route taken by many of the fleeing defeated Royalists and their Parliamentary pursuers into the town.

Start: Stow-on-the-Wold, Market Square, grid ref SP192258

Distance: 5½ miles (8.9km)

Time: 2½ hours

Parking: Stow-on-the-Wold

Refreshments: Pubs and cafes at Stow-on-the-Wold, pub at Broadwell

Map: OS Outdoor Leisure 45 (The Cotswolds)

After Charles I's disastrous defeat at Naseby in 1645, there was very little chance of a Royalist recovery and the king's only hope was for his remaining forces in the Midlands and Welsh Marches to join him at his headquarters at Oxford for one last attempt. Accordingly in early 1646, he ordered Lord Astley to gather these forces and march to Oxford. Parliamentary commanders heard of this move and decided to intercept Astley.

By 20 March, Astley's troops had reached the top of Broadway Hill and were heading towards the important route centre of Stow-on-the-Wold. The pursuing Parliamentary army had watched them climb the hill and continued to follow them. On the following day, Morgan, the Parliamentary commander, decided to confront the enemy on high ground about 2 miles (3.2km) north of Stow and approximately half a mile (0.8km) west of the village of Donnington.

The victorious Parliamentary army pursued the defeated enemy right into the centre of Stow-on-the-Wold and many Royalist soldiers were killed in the Market Square and adjacent streets.

This was open country at the time but Horsington Plantation now occupies part of the battle site.

Compared with Edgehill and Naseby, the encounter was more of a skirmish than a battle. Morgan attacked first but his infantry troops had to clamber up a steep slope and their advance was checked. But the Royalist cavalry retreated at the first Parliamentary cavalry charge and Astley's army was pushed back towards Stow. Pursued by the triumphant Parliamentary troops, the Royalists retreated right into the centre of the town where the fighting and killing continued.

After the battle, many Royalist prisoners were temporarily held in the parish church before being marched to Gloucester. Stow was the last open battle of the Civil War; from then on the main action consisted of the Parliamentarians mopping up the remaining Royalist garrisons throughout the country.

The Route

1. Begin in the large Market Square by the cross and facing the church, turn right. Turn right along a street called Parsons Corner and, at a T-junction, turn left along a lane signposted as a No Through Road. The lane becomes an attractive tree-lined drive, narrows to a path and finally emerges onto a lane. Turn right downhill into Broadwell and, at a T-junction by the spacious green, turn left. Where the lane bends right, bear slightly left along an enclosed path to a gate, go through and keep ahead across a field, later by a wall on the left. Go through a kissing gate into the churchyard and pass to the left of the medieval church. In the churchyard is a fine collection of `wool bale` tombs, so called because they are supposed to represent bales of wool, the mainstay of the medieval Cotswold economy. Go through a gate on the far side, descend steps to a lane and turn right to a T-junction.

2. Turn left, in the Donnington and Moreton-in-Marsh direction, carefully cross the busy A429 and keep ahead into the hamlet of Donnington. Take the first lane on the right, follow the lane to the left in front of the entrance to Donnington Manor and, where it bends left again, turn right along a track.

3. Look out for where you turn left through a waymarked gate and walk along the left edge of a field to a stile. Climb it, keep ahead by a wire fence on the left, climb a stone stile and turn right along the right edge of the next field. Follow the edge to the left and climb a stile in the corner. Ahead is a monument marking the site of the battle. The woodland seen over to the right – Horsington Plantation – was open country at the time and is where the battle began. Bear slightly left, head downhill across the field to a footbridge and stile at the bottom and after climbing the stile, bear right uphill across the next field to a stile in the top corner. Climb it and, at a crossways a few yards ahead, turn left over a stile. Keep by the left edge of a field, passing to the right of barns, go through a gate and keep ahead to the A424. Turn left and take the first lane on the left, signposted to Donnington.

4. On the edge of the village, turn sharp right along a tarmac track, signposted to Holmleigh. The track later becomes a rough enclosed track that ends at a gate. Go through, walk along the left edge of a field, go through another gate and turn left to the A429. Turn right into Stow-on-the-Wold and, at the second set of traffic lights, turn left along High Street back to the Market Square. The victorious Parliamentary army pushed the routed enemy back into Stow and the killing continued right into the Market Square and the adjacent streets, especially Digbeth Street which alleg-

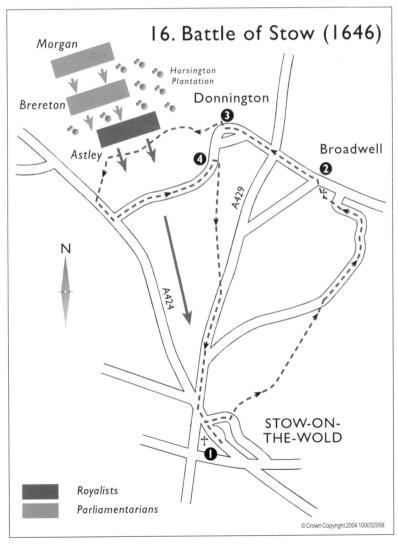

16. Battle of Stow (1646)

Morgan

Horsington Plantation

Brereton

Donnington

Astley

Broadwell

N

A429

A424

STOW-ON-THE-WOLD

Royalists

Parliamentarians

© Crown Copyright 2004 100032058

edly ran with blood. After the battle, around 1500 Royalist prisoners were held in the medieval church before being marched to Gloucester but the only tomb in the church to anyone killed in the battle is that of Captain Hastings Keyt, on the floor of the chancel. A memorial stone to the battle was placed in the churchyard in 1992.

17

The Siege of Newark, 1643-1646

Most of the places in the town centre associated with Newark during the Civil War are visited and there is also an extension to the earthwork of Queen's Sconce on the south side of the town. There is an attractive stretch beside the River Trent, with dramatic views of Newark Castle.

Start: Newark-on-Trent, Market Place, grid ref SK799538

Distance: 2½ miles (4km)

Time: 1½ hours

Parking: Newark-on-Trent

Refreshments: Pubs, restaurants and cafes at Newark

Map: OS Explorer 271 (Newark-on-Trent)

Newark-on-Trent was of considerable importance during the Civil War and the townspeople had to endure three sieges in the space of four years. There are a number of reasons why it was such a key town. It was – and still is – situated at the junction of two major routes – the Great North Road and the Fosse Way – and controlled a crossing point over the River Trent, the traditional boundary between northern and southern England. It was also a strongly Royalist town in an area that was mainly sympathetic to the Parliamentary cause and had a strong castle and defences.

Newark had four governors throughout the Civil War and the first of these, Sir John Henderson, was in charge of the defence of the town during the first siege in 1643. Parliamentary forces besieged the town between 27 and 29 February. Although the attackers had a numerical advantage, the defenders, urged on by Henderson who directed operations from his white horse, forced them to retreat and the town was saved.

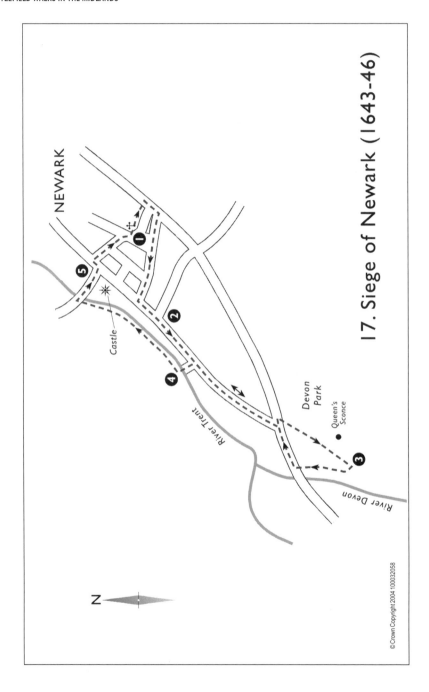

17. Siege of Newark (1643–46)

© Crown Copyright 2004 100032058

In the June of the same year, Charles I's consort, Henrietta Maria, arrived in Newark with an army and stayed there for a while before journeying on to join the king at his Oxford headquarters.

The second siege began on 29 February 1644. A Parliamentary army of around 7000 encircled Newark and bombarded it with cannon. One cannon ball knocked a hole in the church spire, still visible today. Charles I ordered his nephew, Prince Rupert, to come to the relief of the town and, after a rapid march from his headquarters at Chester, Rupert reached the outskirts of Newark on 21 March. In a fierce cavalry battle on Beacon Hill on the east side of the town, Rupert's troops were victorious and the Parliamentary army, led by Sir John Meldrum, surrendered.

The third and final siege was the longest, lasting from November 1645 to May 1646. By the autumn of 1645, the war was going badly for the Royalists and the garrison at Newark was becoming increasingly isolated and vulnerable. Strenuous efforts were made to strengthen the defences in preparation for the attack and two large earthworks, Queen's Sconce and King's Sconce, were constructed outside the main line of defences. During the siege, Newark was surrounded by around 14,000 Scottish and Parliamentary forces and the town was pounded day and night for over 6 months. Resistance was spirited but food was short and by early 1646, the Royalist cause was collapsing throughout the country. On 5 May, Charles I decided to surrender to the Scots at nearby Southwell – he thought he might be able to get a better deal from them than from his Parliamentary enemies – and instructed the Governor of Newark, Lord John Bellasis, to surrender. The surrender documents were signed on 6 May and the garrison was allowed to march out of the town. By this time, plague had broken out in Newark and it has been estimated that around 200 people died from it. The defences and most of the castle were later dismantled by Parliamentary soldiers.

The Route

1. From Newark's handsome and spacious Market Place, dominated by the fine 18th-century Town Hall, make for Stodman Street. On the corner of Stodman Street and the Market Place is a timber-framed Tudor building, the Governor's House, in which the wartime governors of Newark Castle lived. The house was

also the scene of a heated argument between Charles I and his nephew, Prince Rupert, in September 1645 over the running of the war. Continue along Stodman Street to a T-junction and turn left.

2. Where the main road bends left, keep ahead along Millgate to a T-junction. Turn left, then almost immediately turn right, at a public footpath sign, into Devon Park and take the broad, tarmac track that bears slightly right to the Queen's Sconce. This was one of the two new earthworks constructed in 1645 as part of the strengthening and improvement of the town's defences in preparation for an expected artillery onslaught. King's Sconce to the north of the town has disappeared but Queen's Sconce has survived and is one of the most impressive works of its kind anywhere in the country. It was star-shaped and cleverly designed to absorb artillery fire.

3. When you are roughly at the end of the earthworks, turn right onto a path that leads across grass to the River Devon and turn right along its banks to the road again. Turn right, take the first turning on the left (Millgate) and retrace your steps as far as Mill Lane. Turn left along Mill Lane and cross a bridge over the River Trent.

4. Immediately turns right onto a riverside path. After passing Newark Town Lock, turn left to cross a footbridge over another channel of the river and turn right to continue along the riverside path. Pass by the castle walls and bear left up to a road. Turn right to cross the bridge over the river and keep ahead to a T-junction. The entrance to the castle is to the right. Newark Castle was built in the 12th century and was one of the residences of the bishops of Lincoln. King John died here in 1216 after losing the Crown Jewels in The Wash. Throughout the sieges, it was the major target for the Parliamentary attackers and was held by the Royalists until the final surrender in May 1646. After the Civil War, it was dismantled on the orders of Cromwell.

5. Turn left at the T-junction, take the first turning on the right into Kirkgate and walk up to the church. On the way you pass Henrietta Maria's House, two timber-framed Tudor houses in which, according to tradition, Charles I's wife stayed while visit-

Newark's 12th-century castle overlooks the River Trent. During the Civil War, this Royalist stronghold was the principal target for the Parliamentary besiegers.

ing Newark in June 1643. Take the path to the left of the church into gardens and bear left onto another path, which curves left to a lamppost. From this point, look back at the spire and just below a window, a cannon ball hole can be seen, allegedly fired by Cromwell's troops while attacking the castle in 1644. Newark's grand and spacious parish church, one of the finest in the country, was mainly built in the 13th century but the spire was added in the 14th century. After the surrender in 1646, the font was damaged by Parliamentary soldiers. Continue along the path beside the church to a road, turn right and turn right again along Bridge Street to return to the Market Place.

What else is there to see?

Newark Museum, in Appletongate behind the Market Place, has displays on the Civil War in Newark and a model of the town's defences, including a reconstruction of the Queen's Sconce.

18

The Siege of Lichfield, 1643-1646

The atmosphere of tranquillity and elegance that today pervades the close of Lichfield Cathedral makes it difficult to believe that in the 1640s it was under almost constant artillery bombardment which left the cathedral in ruins and destroyed many of the buildings surrounding it. The walk visits the sites connected with the Civil War, plus other places of interest in this small city, and takes you on a circuit of the attractive Stowe Pool to the east of the cathedral.

Start: Lichfield, Market Square, grid ref SK117096

Distance: 2½ miles (4km)

Time: 1½ hours

Parking: Lichfield

Refreshments: Pubs and cafes at Lichfield

Map: OS Explorer 232 (Nuneaton & Tamworth) or town map of Lichfield

Between 1643 and 1646, Lichfield suffered three sieges, two by Parliamentary forces and one by the Royalists. The main military action was concentrated around the cathedral because the close was fortified and during the Civil War was occupied and used as a place of refuge by both Royalist and Parliamentary forces. The Royalists were in occupation for the vast majority of the time: Parliamentary occupation only lasted for a brief period between March and April 1643.

Staffordshire was predominantly Parliamentarian in sympathy but Lichfield, like many cathedral cities, was Royalist. It was roughly in the centre of a narrow belt of Royalist territory that

The ornate west front of Lichfield Cathedral. The fortified close was the principal target during the city's three Civil War sieges and the central spire of the cathedral was shot down.

constituted a vital north-south corridor for the armies of Charles I. Therefore control of the city was important for both sides.

The first siege began on 2 March 1643 when Lord Brooke, a fanatical Puritan, led a Parliamentary assault on the city and the Royalist garrison retreated to the fortified close. On the very first day, Brooke was killed by a sniper on the central spire of the cathedral and on the following day, a Parliamentary force that advanced on the cathedral from St Chad's Church was ambushed in what is now Gaia Lane and forced to retreat. But by 5 March, the Parliamentarians had been reinforced and the Royalists were forced to surrender, mainly because of shortages of both food and ammunition.

This was followed by the brief interlude of Parliamentary occupation, during which the cathedral was ransacked, until a Royalist army, led by Prince Rupert, arrived in Lichfield on 8 April to begin the second siege. An artillery mount – Prince Rupert's Mount – was constructed on the north side of the cathedral and the close was bombarded for almost a fortnight. Again shortage of food and ammunition forced the defenders to surrender on 21 April and Lichfield remained in Royalist hands until almost the end of the war.

The final siege was by far the longest and lasted from 9 March until 10 July 1646. By early 1646, the Royalist cause was virtually lost and Sir William Brereton, Parliamentary commander in Cheshire and another zealous Puritan, was engaged in mopping up the last places of Royalist resistance in the Midlands. He did his job thoroughly. New earthworks were constructed around three sides of the close, which suffered further heavy bombardment. After one particularly intense attack on 12 May, the central spire of the cathedral collapsed. Surrender terms were eventually agreed on 10 July, the siege was lifted and on the following day, the gallant Royalist defenders were allowed to march out of the close.

Many of the buildings in Beacon Street and around the close, including the Bishop's Palace, had been destroyed and the cathedral was left in a very bad state.

The Route

1. Start in the Market Square by Dr Johnson's statue – he was a native of Lichfield – and the 19th-century St Mary's Church, now the Heritage Centre. Walk down Breadmarket Street to the Guildhall; turn right along Bore Street and turn left along St John's Street to St John's Hospital and Chapel. This was originally founded in 1135 to accommodate pilgrims visiting the cathedral but changed its role in 1485 and became a residence for homeless men. It is still inhabited but you can visit the 15th-century chapel.

2. Retrace your steps along St John's Street and keep ahead along Bird Street and Beacon Street. There is a superb view to the right looking across Minster Pool to the three spires of Lichfield Cathedral. To the left is the attractive Beacon Park. During the Civil War, Parliamentary besiegers constructed earthworks here but these are virtually impossible to trace. As you continue along Beacon Street, you pass Milley's Hospital, founded in 1504 as an almshouse for 15 women. Although in the thick of the fighting, it was one of the few buildings to survive the sieges. Turn right by the Little Barrow Hotel into Anson Avenue and turn right along a paved path – Prince Rupert's Way – to Prince Rupert's Mount. Constructed in 1643 by Royalist troops under Rupert's command, it is by far the best-preserved of Lichfield's Civil War defences.

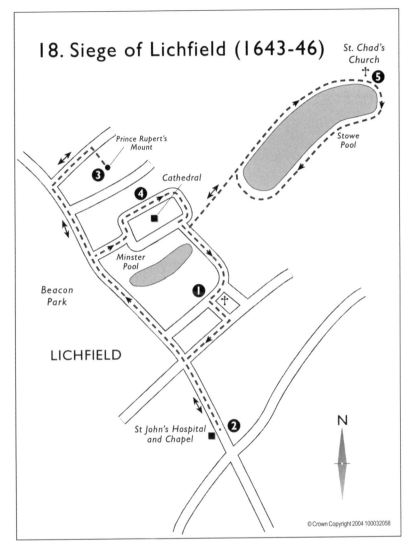

18. Siege of Lichfield (1643-46)

St. Chad's Church

Prince Rupert's Mount

Stowe Pool

Cathedral

Minster Pool

Beacon Park

LICHFIELD

St John's Hospital and Chapel

N

© Crown Copyright 2004 100032058

3. Retrace your steps to Beacon Street, walk down it back towards the city centre and turn left into The Close up to the west front of the cathedral. Lichfield Cathedral was started around the end of the 12th century and was completed in the early 14th century. As well as being one of England's most beautiful cathedrals, it has the distinction of being the only one to possess three spires. It also has the less enviable distinction of being the one that suffered the most damage during the Civil War. The interior was used as a barracks and stables, there was scarcely a roof intact and the central spire was shot down. After the restoration of the monarchy in 1660, it was thoroughly restored and the spire on the central tower rebuilt. Further restoration took place in the 18th and 19th centuries. Apart from the three spires, the chief glories of the cathedral are the ornate west front and the 14th-century Lady Chapel, which contains 16th-century glass brought from a Belgian monastery.

4. Turn left and right to walk along the north side of the close. If you take a look in Vicars Close, just off the north west corner, there are some old, timber-framed buildings that survived the siege. The Bishop's Palace in the north east corner was not so lucky and was rebuilt in 1687. Follow the road around the east end of the cathedral, turn left and take the first turning on the left, a tarmac track called Reeve Lane, for a circuit of Stowe Pool. Continue along a path, which curves right around the edge of the pool to St Chad's Church. A Saxon church was founded on this site in the 7th century by St Chad, the first bishop of Lichfield. The present church dates mainly from the 13th century but had to be restored in the 17th century following extensive damage in the Civil War – hence the brickwork in the upper part of the nave. During the siege of Lichfield, the church was a military storehouse and was used as a base for a Parliamentary attack on the close in March 1643.

5. Complete the circuit of Stowe Pool, retrace your steps along Reeve Lane and turn left into Dam Street. Look out for a plaque above No 24 (Brooke House) which records that it was here that the Parliamentary commander, Lord Brooke, was killed by a Royalist sniper firing from the central spire of the cathedral. Pass the end of Minster Pool on the right and the street leads back to the Market Square.

What else is there to see?

The Lichfield Heritage Centre, housed in the former St Mary's Church, has displays on the Civil War.

19

The Battle of Worcester, 3 September 1651

The battle site covers a large area, stretching from the riverside meadows bordering the Severn and Teme on the south side of Worcester to the heart of the city itself and much of it is now covered by suburban expansion. As well as a tour of the city, visiting places associated with the battle, the walk takes you along the east bank of the Severn to its confluence with the Teme. From here, you overlook open meadows on the west bank of the river, the most undisturbed part of the battlefield.

Start: Worcester, the Guildhall, grid ref SO850547

Distance: 4½ miles (7.2km)

Time: 2 hours

Parking: Worcester

Refreshments: Pubs and cafes at Worcester

Map: OS Explorer 204 (Worcester & Droitwich Spa)

In 1649, the English Parliament executed Charles I and abolished the monarchy. But north of the border, the Scottish Parliament proclaimed his son King Charles II and a Scottish army prepared to help him regain his English throne. Embarking on a pre-emptive strike, Cromwell marched into Scotland and defeated Charles at Dunbar in September 1650. This was followed by almost a year of skirmishing between the two sides in Scotland but in August 1651, Charles II crossed the border into England and prepared to march on London.

The Scottish army was led by the Duke of Hamilton and David Leslie. As it made its way through north-west England, Charles hoped to acquire English allies but by the time the exhausted troops arrived at Worcester, he had not gained as much support as he had expected. Charles had about 16,000 men but Cromwell, who had followed him down the east side of the country, had almost double that number with around 28,000.

Charles chose to stop at Worcester because he hoped for some reinforcements to arrive from Wales and because the city had an excellent defensive position, protected by the rivers Severn and Teme and with the sconce, or defensive earthwork, of Fort Royal on its south east side. For additional protection, Charles destroyed the nearby bridges over both rivers and placed guns on Fort Royal.

Cromwell did not just want a victory; he desired the complete destruction of the Royalist forces and the end of any possible threat of a restoration of the monarchy. His strategy was to split his army into two. One army, led by Charles Fleetwood and John Lambert, attacked the Royalists and Scots across the meadows on the west side of the Severn; the other – led by himself – advanced on Worcester along the east bank. In order that the armies could cross the rivers and maintain communication with each other afterwards, he ordered the construction of a bridge of boats across both the Teme and Severn.

Although Fleetwood and Lambert encountered stiff resistance, the numerical advantage of the Parliamentary forces showed as their armies pushed the Scots and Royalists back across the riverside meadows towards the city. From the tower of the cathedral, Charles watched the defeat of his armies but, noticing that the Parliamentary forces were divided into two groups, he decided to launch a major attack on Cromwell himself. Despite fighting bravely and making some initial headway as far as Red Hill (now covered by suburban housing and roads), Cromwell's forces finally pushed him and his troops back into the streets of Worcester after several hours of heavy fighting.

As darkness fell, the remnants of Leslie's cavalry fled and the abandoned Royalist infantry were left to their fate. Many were taken prisoner but many more were butchered in the narrow streets of Worcester. Few escaped, apart from Charles himself who slipped out of the city.

It was a complete rout and Cromwell had achieved his aim. The Civil War was finally over and the Royalist cause was lost. After his

Worcester Cathedral from the Civil War defence of Fort Royal to the south-east. Charles II surveyed the battle from the cathedral tower.

escape from Worcester, Charles II managed to avoid capture, despite several close calls, and went into exile on the continent. For the next nine years Great Britain, for the only time in its history, was a republic.

The Route

1. The walk starts in front of the ornate, early 18th-century Guildhall. There are statues of both Charles I and Charles II on either side of the entrance, symbolising the loyalty of the city to the Royalist cause. With your back to the building, turn left along High Street and turn right into Church Street. Keep ahead along Mealcheapen Street into the Cornmarket and turn right into New Street. On the left is King Charles's House, built in 1577. It was from here that Charles II escaped after his defeat in the battle.

Walk along New Street, continue along picturesque Friar Street and, at a T-junction, turn left into Sidbury. After crossing City Walls Road and a canal bridge, you reach the Commandery. This fine 15th-century, timber-framed building served as Charles's headquarters during the battle and now houses a fascinating and detailed exhibition about the battle and Civil War.

2. At this point make a brief detour to Fort Royal: keep ahead along Sidbury, turn left into Wylds Lane and then right beside a barrier, up steps and across grass to the top. From this massive earthwork or sconce, built to defend the city, there is a magnificent view over Worcester and the surrounding countryside, with the Malvern Hills prominent on the horizon. Charles II placed guns here in 1651 in an attempt to keep Cromwell's armies at bay.

Retrace your steps to the Commandery, turn right beside it, turn left to the canal towpath, turn left again along it and descend steps to pass under the road bridge. Follow the towpath of the Worcester and Birmingham Canal to Diglis Basins and, where the path ends at a parking area, turn right between the canal basins. Cross a footbridge, keep ahead, turn right over another footbridge and turn left alongside the canal again at Diglis Top Lock.

At Diglis Bottom Lock, turn left onto a riverside path beside the Severn, cross a footbridge over another basin and keep ahead along a short stretch of road. After passing Diglis Lock, the route continues along a riverside path again. Follow the path, looking out for the regular Severn Way signs, as far as the confluence of the Severn and Teme, seen on the opposite bank.

3. You have to look carefully as the Teme is narrow here and the view is partially obscured by bushes along the riverbank. It was close to this point that Cromwell built his 'bridge of boats' across both rivers in order that his forces on both banks of the Severn could maintain communication. Retrace your steps to the Diglis Basin but instead of following the canal, cross a footbridge over it and continue along an attractive, tarmac riverside path to the cathedral.

4. At the corner of a wall, turn right through a gate, turn left up steps and turn right to walk through College Green on the south side of the cathedral. Worcester Cathedral was built mainly between 1170 and 1374 and its 14th-century tower rises majestically above the Severn. It was from the top of this tower that Charles II watched his armies being defeated and it is still a superb vantage

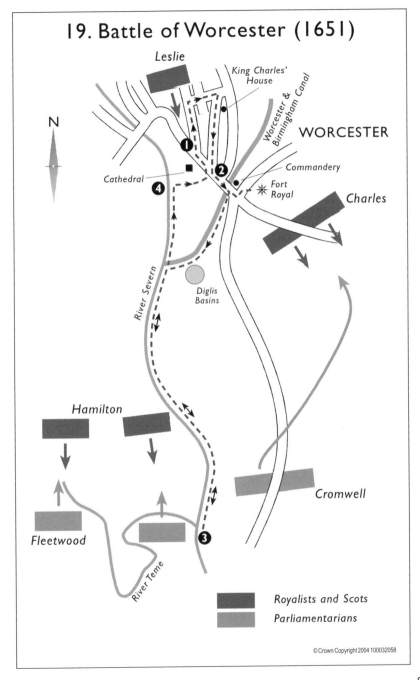

19. Battle of Worcester (1651)

Leslie

King Charles' House

Worcester & Birmingham Canal

WORCESTER

N

Cathedral

Commandery

Fort Royal

Charles

River Severn

Diglis Basins

Hamilton

Cromwell

Fleetwood

River Teme

Royalists and Scots

Parliamentarians

© Crown Copyright 2004 100032058

point from which to view the site of the battle. Inside the cathedral are the tombs of King John and Arthur, Prince of Wales, elder brother of Henry VIII and first husband of Catherine of Aragon. Pass under the Edgar Tower, turn left up steps and walk along a path to the east end of the cathedral. Turn left along College Street and then turn right, passing the statue of Sir Edward Elgar, along the pedestrianised High Street back to the Guildhall.

20

Charles II at Boscobel House, September 1651

The walk follows in some of the footsteps of Charles II as he made his way across the Midlands trying to escape from Cromwell's pursuers after his defeat at the battle of Worcester. Much of it is on the well-waymarked Monarch's Way, a meandering long distance route from the Midlands to the south coast that traces the deposed king's likely route to exile.

Start: Boscobel House, signposted from A5 just to the east of Weston-under-Lizard, grid ref SJ837084

Distance: 5½ miles (8.9km)

Time: 2½ hours

Parking: Park on the grass verge in front of Boscobel House not in the English Heritage car park, which is for visitors to the house

Refreshments: Pub at Bishops Wood, café at Boscobel House

Map: OS Explorer 242 (Telford, Ironbridge and The Wrekin)

After his defeat at the battle of Worcester on 3 September 1651, Charles II was forced to go on the run, pursued by Cromwell's forces. He was keen to make for London but was advised that Scotland would be safer and headed northwards. After riding through the night, he arrived at White Ladies near Boscobel, a house built on the site of a medieval nunnery. Both White Ladies and Boscobel were owned by Francis Cotton, a Royalist supporter, but he was not in residence at the time. Instead the king was looked after by four brothers, the Penderels. One of them, Richard Penderel, hid with him in a nearby wood, Spring Coppice, for a while when Cromwell's soldiers were in the vicinity.

After his defeat at the Battle of Worcester in 1651, Charles II stayed at Boscobel House while on the run from Cromwell's troops. He had to spend most of one day hidden in a nearby oak tree.

It was while at White Ladies that Charles changed his mind and decided to make for London via Wales, where he had supporters. Disguised as a country yokel, he and Richard Penderel set out westwards to cross the River Severn and on the way he may have stayed for a short time at Richard's cottage, Hubbal Grange, about 1 mile (1.6km) away.

The crossings of the Severn were so closely guarded that Charles was forced to change his plans and he retraced his steps, this time staying at Boscobel House. He was not able to stay long in the house as the whole area was swarming with Cromwell's soldiers and he was forced to seek refuge in a nearby oak tree. He stayed hidden in the tree for most of the day – 6 September – and did not come down and return to the house until after dark.

After a reasonably comfortable night at Boscobel House, he departed on the evening of the following day (7 September) for Moseley Hall near Wolverhampton, another Royalist safe house. He journeyed on to Bristol and then to the south coast. From there he sailed to exile in France and remained in exile until his recall to the throne in 1660.

The Route

1. The main claim to fame of Boscobel House, a modest but pictur-esque early 17th-century timber-framed house, is the temporary refuge it provided for Charles II in September 1651. Like most Catholic houses at the time, it has the usual priest holes and secret hiding places. There is an attractive garden and most visi-tors take the short walk to the Royal Oak, recently battered some-what by storms. It is probably a descendant of the oak tree in which the king hid, as the original was largely destroyed by over-zealous souvenir hunters.

   Start the walk by turning right along a lane to a T-junction and turn left. At a yellow waymark, turn along the track to Pearse Hay Farm and, just after passing a barn, turn left along an enclosed track to a road.

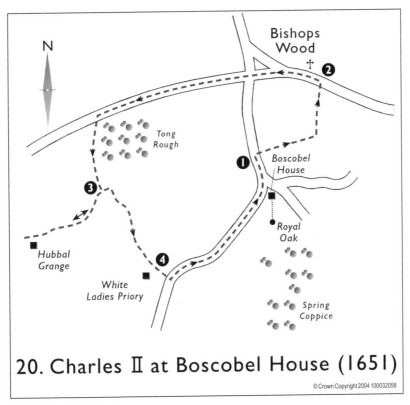

20. Charles II at Boscobel House (1651)

© Crown Copyright 2004 100032058

2. Turn left, passing Bishops Wood Church. At a fork, take the left-hand lane, signposted to Tong and Codsall. At a crossroads turn right for the pub but the route continues ahead and after about three-quarters of a mile (1.2km), turn left at the corner of a wood (Tong Rough) along a tarmac track.

3. At a T-junction, the main route continues to the left but turn right along a track for a short detour to the scanty and overgrown remains of Hubbal Grange, Richard Penderel's cottage where Charles may have stopped for a short while en route for the River Severn. These will be found at a meeting of tracks just beyond a waymarked post. Retrace your steps to the tarmac track and follow it around a right bend to Meashill Farm. Turn left through a gate in front of the farmhouse, follow the edge of the farmyard to the right and right again – the route is well waymarked – and turn left along an enclosed path. Continue gently downhill along the left edge of a field and in the corner, go through a gate and keep ahead through a belt of trees to the ruins of White Ladies Priory.

4. The house which, like Boscobel, gave shelter to the king in September 1651, has entirely disappeared. What you see now are the ruins of the small, 12th-century nunnery, which preceded it on the site. Continue along the tree-lined path to a lane, turn left and follow it for almost 1 mile (1.6km) back to the start.

21

Bonnie Prince Charlie at Derby, December 1745

It is unfortunate that most of the buildings in Derby that have links with the brief Jacobite occupation of the town in 1745 have been demolished, including Exeter House, the temporary headquarters of Bonnie Prince Charlie. The walk begins in the large Market Place, the main assembly point for the Jacobites, takes you through the attractive Riverside Gardens and includes many of Derby's historic monuments.

Start: Derby, Market Place, grid ref SK354364

Distance: 2 miles (3.2km)

Time: 1 hour

Parking: Plenty of car parks in Derby city centre but best to use the Park and Ride scheme

Refreshments: Pubs, restaurants and cafés at Derby

Map: OS Explorer 259 (Derby & Uttoxeter) or town map of Derby

The Glorious Revolution of 1688-89 resulted in the deposition of the Catholic James II and his replacement by his Protestant son-in-law and daughter, William III and Mary II. In order to prevent the future possibility of a Catholic coming to the throne, the English Parliament passed the Act of Settlement in 1701 which stated that after William and Mary and James's younger daughter, Anne, the succession should pass to the nearest Protestant relations, the German House of Hanover. Therefore, James II's son, James Edward Stuart, the Old Pretender, and his successors were barred from the throne and on the death of Queen Anne in 1714, the Elector of Hanover duly became King George I.

The Jacobite Rebellion of 1715 was an attempt by James and his supporters to seize the throne from the newly-installed Hanoverians but was unsuccessful. Thirty years later, his son, Charles Edward Stuart, the Young Pretender, better known as Bonnie Prince Charlie, made another attempt on behalf of his father. Conditions seemed favourable. Government forces were involved in a continental and colonial war with France and the Young Pretender was promised French aid.

Charles landed on the west coast of Scotland on 25 July and the Highlands rallied to his cause. By the middle of September he was in Edinburgh and defeated a Government army at Prestonpans. Seemingly in control of Scotland, he now decided to invade England in November and march on London. He captured Carlisle and continued southwards, through Lancaster, Preston and Manchester and on into the Midlands. Everywhere he received outwardly enthusiastic receptions but little support.

Derby, which was entered on 4 December, was no different. Although largely Hanoverian in sympathy, the townspeople gave him a great welcome. Church bells were rung, bonfires were lit and a local tax raised £3,000 for the Jacobites. On 5 December, a service was held in All Saints' Church, now the cathedral. But attempts to recruit from the local gentry were unsuccessful. Disappointed by the lukewarm support in England, his commanders, especially Lord George Murray, were becoming increasingly alarmed by reports that the Duke of Cumberland was advancing northwards with an army and that other large Hanoverian forces were assembling to defend London.

A stormy debate was held to discuss whether to continue towards London or return to Scotland. Murray strongly advised the latter option and, although Charles himself disagreed and felt both bitter and betrayed by his cautious commanders, he had no alternative but to go along with them. By dawn on 6 December, the Jacobite army slipped out of Derby and started to retrace its steps northwards.

The Route

1. The walk begins in the large, open Market Place, where the Jacobite army assembled on 4 December 1745 after their arrival in the town. Facing the 19th-century Guildhall, turn left and cross

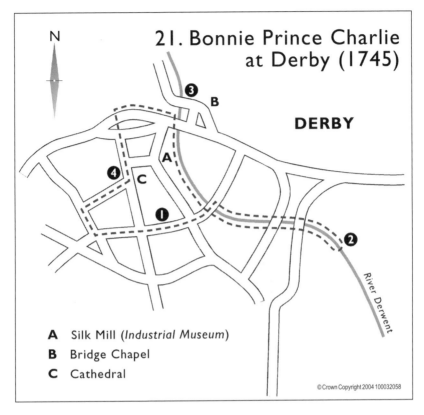

21. Bonnie Prince Charlie at Derby (1745)

N

DERBY

River Derwent

A Silk Mill (*Industrial Museum*)
B Bridge Chapel
C Cathedral

© Crown Copyright 2004 100032058

Full Street. Near the corner of Full Street and Derwent Street stood Exeter House, Charles's headquarters in 1745. The house was demolished in 1854. Keep ahead along Derwent Street and immediately after crossing Exeter Bridge over the River Derwent, bear right onto a paved path across the Riverside Gardens. Pass under a modern road bridge and, where the path ends, continue along a road, passing in front of the offices of the Derby Evening Telegraph.

2. Turn right to cross a footbridge over the river, turn right again and follow a path along the other bank of the Derwent, passing in front of the Council House, back to Exeter Bridge. Cross the road and continue along the riverside path towards the Industrial Museum. Across the grass to the left is a statue of Bonnie Prince Charlie, with the cathedral beyond. Derby Industrial Museum occupies the site of what is regarded as the first factory in England, Lombe's Silk Mill, built between 1717 and 1721. A fire in 1910 destroyed most of the original building but it was rebuilt on similar lines.

Continue past the Industrial Museum and pass under – in quick succession – a modern bridge and an older bridge, the latter completed in 1794. Just beyond the second bridge, turn sharp left to the Chapel of St Mary on the Bridge.

The statue to Bonnie Prince Charlie stands near the east end of Derby Cathedral. During their short stay in 1745, a service was held for the Jacobites in the cathedral, then a parish church.

3. This is one of only five surviving bridge chapels in England and dates from the 13th and 14th centuries. Turn right in front of the chapel, cross Sowter Road and keep ahead along a path, parallel to the inner bypass, to St Mary's Roman Catholic church. In front of the church, turn left to cross a footbridge over the bypass, follow the path to left and right and pass under a subway. Turn right at a T-junction and then continue along Queen Street, passing Ye Olde Dolphine Inn, dating from 1530 and Derby's oldest inn, to the cathedral.

4. Apart from the imposing west tower – the only survivor of an early 16th-century church – Derby Cathedral is a fine Classical building built in 1723-25 and extended in the late 20th century. It

was originally the parish church of All Saints and was elevated to cathedral status in 1927. Bonnie Prince Charlie attended a service in the church on 5 December, an event marked by a stone on the wall of the nave. Turn right along St Mary's Gate and, at a T-junction, turn left along Bold Lane. At a fork by the Museum and Art Gallery, bear left along Sadler Gate. This is likely to be the route that the Jacobite troops took in December 1745 to get to the Market Place and it returns you to the start.

What else is there to see?

There is a Bonnie Prince Charlie Room in Derby Museum and Art Gallery.

22

The Bombing of Coventry, November 1940

Coventry was very much a battlefield in November 1940, as much of the centre of the city was destroyed during an exceptionally heavy bombing raid. The walk takes you on a circuit of the city centre, highlighting both the older buildings – including some outstanding medieval ones – that fortunately survived the destruction and some of the post-war redevelopments.

Start: Coventry, Broadgate, grid ref SP334790

Distance: 2 miles (3.2km)

Time: 1 hour

Parking: Plenty of car parks in Coventry city centre but best to use the Park and Ride scheme

Refreshments: Pubs and cafes in Coventry

Map: OS 221 (Coventry & Warwick) or town map of Coventry

On the night of 14-15 November 1940, Coventry suffered the worst single air raid of any British city during World War II. It lasted eleven hours and left most of the city centre in ruins.

At the start of its bombing raids on Britain, the German air force concentrated on the capital, the airfields and the ports but in the autumn of 1940 it turned to the great armament manufacturing cities of the Midlands – Birmingham, Coventry and Wolverhampton. The aim was to deal a crippling blow to the British armaments industry before American help started to tilt the scales in Britain's favour.

Before the war, Coventry was a maze of narrow streets with many

The ruins of the old cathedral were retained and adjoin the new Coventry Cathedral that was completed in 1962.

old buildings and fine churches, a reflection of its importance as one of the largest towns in England during the Middle Ages and after. Wool had been its major industry at that time but during the Victorian era engineering industries had been set up and in the 1920s and 30s the city had become an important centre for the motor vehicle industry. Since the outbreak of the war, many of Coventry's large firms – Vickers Armstrong, Hawker Siddeley, Rolls-Royce, Alvis, Rootes, Daimler, Courtaulds – had turned to producing munitions, military vehicles and other war materials and were an obvious target for the Luftwaffe. However the massive and devastating attack of 14 November – codenamed Operation Moonlight Sonata – took both the government in London and the citizens of Coventry by surprise.

The blitz started at around 7pm with incendiary raids and this was followed by the dropping of high explosive bombs. Despite many acts of individual heroism, the intensity and length of the raid made it impossible for the emergency services to cope as the city burned around them. By the time the raid ended around 6 am on the following morning, over 30,000 incendiary bombs and 500 tons of high explosive had fallen on Coventry. Around 60,000 buildings, including the cathedral, had been destroyed or severely damaged, at least 568 people were killed and over 1200 injured.

Most large British cities had to endure bombing raids and suffered a great deal of destruction during the war – and Coventry itself had further attacks – but nothing on the scale experienced on that terrible night in November 1940.

The Route

1. Start by the statue to Lady Godiva and, with your back to the Cathedral Lanes Shopping Centre, turn left. Turn left again and, almost immediately, turn right along Greyfriars Lane to Ford's Hospital. Although these Tudor almshouses – endowed in 1509 – were damaged by the bombing, this outstanding building was rebuilt using original timbers in the early 1950s. From here keep ahead, crossing Barracks Way, to the tower and spire of Greyfriars church. This spire has survived both the demolition of the original Franciscan friary, suppressed by Henry VIII in 1542, and the destruction of its successor, Christchurch, which was burnt down, not in the main bombing raid in November 1940 but during a later one in April 1941. Since 1974, the surrounding area has been named Dresden Place as a symbol of the friendship between the two cities created out of mutual wartime destruction.

2. Walk along Warwick Road and turn right into Greyfriars Road, which curves right. Continue along what is now Queen Victoria Road to St John's Church, a 15th-century building that was used as a prison for Royalist prisoners in the Civil War. Coventry was a staunchly Parliamentarian town and the hostility shown to the prisoners is the origin of the phrase 'to be sent to Coventry'. In front of the church, turn left and walk along Spon Street, lined by medieval buildings, most of which have been re-erected here from other parts of the city. Retrace your steps, pass in front of the church and immediately turn left along Hill Street to Bonds Hospital. These Tudor almshouses, later used as a school, are grouped around an attractive courtyard. On the night of the blitz in November 1940, one elderly resident helped to prevent the buildings from burning down by putting out incendiaries with sand.

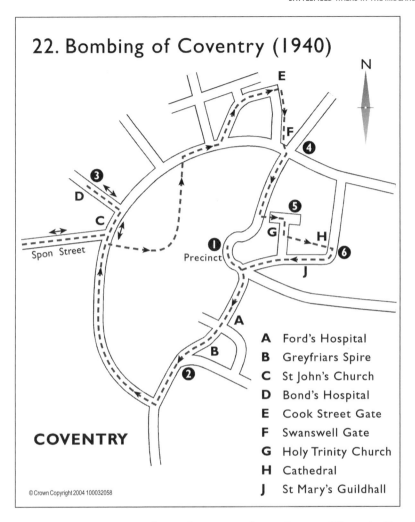

22. Bombing of Coventry (1940)

N

Spon Street

Precinct

COVENTRY

© Crown Copyright 2004 100032058

A   Ford's Hospital
B   Greyfriars Spire
C   St John's Church
D   Bond's Hospital
E   Cook Street Gate
F   Swanswell Gate
G   Holy Trinity Church
H   Cathedral
J   St Mary's Guildhall

3. Retrace your steps a short distance along Queen Victoria Road, turn left into the glass-covered Lower Precinct and turn left again into Smithfold Way. The Lower Precinct is new but the Upper Precinct, built after the war, was one of the first pedestrianised shopping areas in Britain, pioneering the then revolutionary concepts of separating people from traffic and having shops on two levels. On emerging into Corporation Street turn right, turn left into Bishop Street and immediately bear right along Silver Street. Pass the Museum of Road Transport, continue along Cook

113

Street and go through Cook Street Gate. This and Swanswell Gate are the only two remaining gates in Coventry's medieval walls. Between them is the longest stretch of the wall, which you walk alongside as you turn right onto a gently descending path through Lady Herbert's Garden to emerge onto a road by Swanswell Gate.

4. Turn right, keep ahead up Trinity Street and turn left up steps into cobbled Priory Row. The 15th-century cottages on the left survived the war, as did the 18th-century houses further on. Also on the left are the excavated remains of the medieval priory, Coventry's first cathedral, originally founded in the 11th century by Leofric and Godiva and destroyed during Henry VIII's dissolution of the monasteries. To the right is the fine Holy Trinity Church, founded in the 12th century, which also miraculously survived the blitz.

5. Turn right into Cuckoo Lane and turn left into St Michael's Lane to the cathedral, passing between the ruins of the old cathedral and its modern successor. The cathedral, the major casualty of that night in November 1940, was a grand 15th-century parish church elevated to cathedral status with the founding of a new diocese of Coventry in 1918. All that survived were the outer walls and – fortunately – the magnificent tower and spire. When the new cathedral was built, the ruins of the old were retained and aligned at right angles to the new one. The new cathedral was completed in 1962 and its most outstanding features are Epstein's sculpture of St Michael the Archangel on the outside and Sutherland's tapestry of Christ, which dominates the interior.

6. Turn right and follow the road around a right bend to St Mary's Guildhall. This rare and superb example of a medieval guildhall dates from the 14th century. Although damaged during the war, it emerged largely unscathed. Continue along Bayley Lane and Pepper Lane to a T-junction, turn right and then right again to return to the start.

Also of interest:

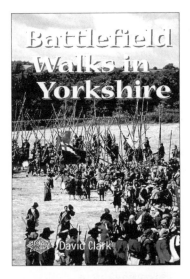

BATTLEFIELD WALKS IN YORKSHIRE

David Clark

Discover the fascination of battlefield exploration whilst appreciating the picturesque and varied terrain of this county, already a walkers' favourite. History comes to life with this companion guide to the battlefields of Yorkshire. Visit sites from the Battle of Heathfield in 633, through the War of the Roses and the English Civil War, to military airfields of the Second World War. Each chapter contains a stimulating account of each battle with up-to-date information on access and facilities. Not only battlefields but sieges (town walks) and military airfields too. Yorkshire is of particular significance, because it contains more important battlefields than any other county, encompassing over one thousand years of English history. *£6.95*

SHROPSHIRE WALKS WITH GHOSTS & LEGENDS

Dorothy Nicolle

Each one of over 20 walks has a particular local legend or ghost story to add that extra something to interest walkers of all ages. There are details of sites well worth exploring throughout Shropshire, many thought to be haunted by ghosts good and bad, ancient and modern!

The walks take you to the many and varied types of countryside found in the county of Shropshire – hills and valleys, towns and villages.

Accompanying each walk are route plans, detailed directions, photographs and the all-important refreshment opportunities, offering a choice of convenient stops en route. Dorothy Nicolle is a Blue Badge guide and lives in the heart of Shropshire. *£7.95*

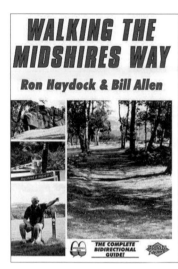

WALKING THE MIDSHIRES WAY

Ron Haydock

The Midshires Way is a 225-mile (360km) footpath and bridleway across Middle England, linking the Ridgeway in Buckinghamshire with the Trans-Pennine Trail at Stockport in Greater Manchester. It passes through the counties of Buckinghamshire, Northamptonshire, Leicestershire, Nottinghamshire, Derbyshire, and the metropolitan area of Greater Manchester.

The Way is divided into 17 sections (each between 10 and 14 miles - a nominal day's walk) with detailed descriptions of readily available accommodation at the end of each section. There is also information about how the Way came into being, the terrain, route descriptions, sketch maps, illustrations and advice for cyclists and equestrians. *£7.95*

LITERARY STROLLS AROUND THE COTSWOLDS & FOREST OF DEAN

Gordon Ottewell

A collection of 40 delightful short strolls with special appeal to lovers of literature and landscape.

All less than three miles in length, the routes spread right across the delightful Cotswold countryside and encourage strollers to find out more about the area through the discovery of its many-faceted literary associations. An original approach to walking which will appeal equally to lovers of literature and landscape.

"With inspirations like J.M. Barrie (Peter Pan), Mary Shelley (Frankenstein), Jane Austen and Dennis Potter, the variety is all-encompassing" COTSWOLD LIFE

£6.95

All of our books are available through booksellers. In case of difficulty, or for a free catalogue, please contact: SIGMA LEISURE, 5 ALTON ROAD, WILMSLOW, CHESHIRE SK9 5DY.

Phone or Fax: 01625-531035   *E-mail:* info@sigmapress.co.uk
Web site and on-line catalogue: www.sigmapress.co.uk